T0360467

Renminbi from Marketization to Internationalization

This study looks into the significance of a floating exchange rate regime, further development of the foreign exchange derivatives market, and concurrent internationalization of the Renminbi (RMB) for a resilient, open, and growing Chinese economy.

The first chapter analyzes the macroeconomic impact of foreign exchange intervention based on empirical studies on 26 economies, explaining why most countries favor a floating exchange rate regime under the existing international monetary system. The second chapter discusses the macroeconomic and microeconomic conditions that would facilitate a successful transition to a floating exchange rate. The final two chapters discuss the importance of further developing the foreign exchange derivatives market in China and explores paths toward further opening-up of the capital market and internationalization of the RMB under a floating exchange rate. Based on the authors' decades of reflection and systematic analysis on real cases both in China and abroad, the title sheds lights on China's exchange rate issues and research on exchange rate policy.

This book will be an essential reference for scholars, students, professionals, and policymakers interested in exchange rate, currency internationalization, the financial market, especially the derivatives market, and the Chinese economy.

Zhongxia Jin has been executive director for China at the International Monetary Fund since 2015 and previously served as head of the Research Institute of the People's Bank of China. His areas of research cover international finance, monetary policy, international trade and investment, international economic governance, and RMB internationalization.

Yue Zhao currently works at the International Monetary Fund. Previously she was an economist at the People's Bank of China. Her areas of research include monetary policy, international finance, and financial regulation.

Haobin Wang currently works at the Ministry of Finance of China. Previously he was an economist at the International Monetary Fund. His areas of research include monetary policy, international finance, and financial regulation.

中国金融四十人论坛
CHINA FINANCE 40 FORUM

China Finance 40 Forum (CF40) is a non-governmental, non-profit and independent think tank dedicated to policy research in the fields of macro economics and finance. CF40 operates as a "40×40 club" with about 40 influential experts around age 40.

The "China Finance 40 Forum Books" focuses on the macroeconomic and financial field with a special emphasis on financial policy studies to facilitate innovations in financial thinking and inspire breakthroughs, while building a high-end, authentic brand for think tank books with top academic quality and policy value.

The "China Finance 40 Forum Books" has published more than 50 monographs and article collections in Chinese since 2009. Through its rigorous and cutting-edge research, this book series has a remarkable reputation in the industry and a broad influence overall.

Regulating China's Shadow Banks
Qingmin Yan and Jianhua Li

A Research on China's Economic Growth Potential
Chong-en Bai and Qiong Zhang

Financing China's Belt and Road Initiative
Investments and Infrastructure
Xiao Gang

Renminbi from Marketization to Internationalization
Zhongxia Jin, Yue Zhao, and Haobin Wang

For more information about this series, please visit: www.routledge.com/China-Finance-40-Forum-Books/book-series/CF40B

Renminbi from Marketization to Internationalization

Zhongxia Jin, Yue Zhao, and Haobin Wang

LONDON AND NEW YORK

First published in English 2022
by Routledge
4 Park Square, Milton Park, Abingdon, Oxon OX14 4RN

and by Routledge
605 Third Avenue, New York, NY 10158

Routledge is an imprint of the Taylor & Francis Group, an informa business

British Library Cataloguing-in-Publication Data
A catalogue record for this book is available from the British Library

Library of Congress Cataloging-in-Publication Data
Names: Jin, Zhongxia, author. | Zhao, Yue, 1988– author. |
Wang, Haobin, 1990– author.
Title: Renminbi from marketization to internationalization /
Zhongxia Jin, Yue Zhao, Haobin Wang.
Description: Milton Park, Abingdon, Oxon;
New York, NY: Routledge, 2022. |
Series: China finance 40 forum books |
Includes bibliographical references and index.
Identifiers: LCCN 2022003508 (print) | LCCN 2022003509 (ebook) |
ISBN 9781032305509 (hardback) | ISBN 9781032305516 (paperback) |
ISBN 9781003305668 (ebook)
Subjects: LCSH: Renminbi–China. | Foreign exchange–China. |
China–Economic conditions.
Classification: LCC HG1285 .J56913 2022 (print) | LCC HG1285 (ebook) |
DDC 332.4/951–dc23/eng/20220126
LC record available at https://lccn.loc.gov/2022003508
LC ebook record available at https://lccn.loc.gov/2022003509

ISBN: 978-1-032-30550-9 (hbk)
ISBN: 978-1-032-30551-6 (pbk)
ISBN: 978-1-003-30566-8 (ebk)

DOI: 10.4324/9781003305668

Typeset in Times New Roman
by Newgen Publishing UK

Contents

Figures

Tables

Preface

As the world ushers in an era of profound changes unseen in decades, the challenges and policy choices China faces have become increasingly complicated. In recent years, tensions between China and the US have gradually escalated to a trade and technology war, and on to a limited financial war, all of which have significantly reshaped the external landscape of China.

The higher tariffs, technology blockade, and financial sanctions that the US imposed on China have exacerbated China's trade and investment environment. Not only can China no longer rely on a persistent current account surplus or the sustained accumulation of foreign reserves to support external investment, but it also has to be able to adjust to all sorts of external shocks quickly and effectively.

The exclusion of China in several recently formed regional trade agreements has meant that China is confronted with a global market that has become increasingly exclusive and segmented across major trade blocs. To make matters worse, the outbreak of the COVID-19 pandemic expedited adjustments in the global supply chains and put many of China's key trading partners in economic and debt constraints, further obstructing China's efforts to expand its global market and assimilate into the global system of resource allocation and specialization. Without proactively rising to these challenges, China risks being forced onto an inward- and backward-looking path with closed-door policies, which will again lead nowhere but to a dead end. The formation of the Regional Comprehensive Economic Partnership (RCEP) and the signing of the Sino-EU investment agreement were major developments against these challenges. The two agreements have strengthened the basis for regional and interregional trade and investment integration, but they have only alleviated rather than eliminated the daunting challenges.

As the Chinese economy becomes increasingly integrated with the global economy, it will need to open up its financial market and capital account further and develop its own global financial center, a network of global financial institutions, and a cross-border payment system. China's long dependence on an international financial system dominated by a reserve currency has made it particularly susceptible to international financial sanctions, including risks of being excluded from the global payment system and being cut off from cross-border trade and financial transactions. The current monetary and financial system in China still lacks the capacity to guarantee full support for cross-border trade and investment in the face of external risks, exposing a weakness that urgently needs to be addressed.

It is also worth noting that China's balance of payments has becomerelatively balanced in recent years. As China's savings rate continues to decline and its capital market continues to open up, its current and capital accounts will likely evolve into a pattern of dynamic balance with deficits and surpluses alternating randomly. Another challenge China faces is whether it should alter the old approach of maintaining current account surpluses and restricting capital account transactions.

To address these challenges, China needs to tap into its enormous domestic market base and further expand its global market share by enhancing its monetary and production capacity. The Chinese government has recently put in motion a new "dual circulation" strategy that emphasizes "internal circulation" as the core with complementary support from "external circulation".

As China strengthens its internal circulation and proactively expands the space for global economic partnership, it also needs to stay vigilant against external risks that may result from economic, financial, and geopolitical conflicts. Market reactions and adjustments to external shocks will be collectively reflected in the exchange rate. In designing its exchange rate policy, should China push ahead with its foreign exchange market reform, and support the integration of internal and external circulations with RMB as the intermediate currency? Or should China intensify its intervention in the foreign exchange market while backing off from its reform efforts and delaying the internationalization of the RMB out of "fear of floating", "fear of exchange rate overshooting", and "fear of capital flight"?

This book emphasizes that a floating exchange rate regime, further development of the foreign exchange derivatives market, and the concurrent internationalization of the RMB are the only ways to navigate severe external challenges and successfully achieve the "dual circulation". Only a floating exchange rate can promptly respond to external shocks and balance-of-payments imbalances and, therefore, function as a shock absorber. Only with a floating exchange rate can China avoid unsustainable intervention with reserve currencies issued by other countries as well as capital controls that would severely impair trade and capital transactions. Only with further relaxation of foreign exchange controls can China fully develop its onshore international financial centers to facilitate the use of the RMB for both the current and capital accounts and make the RMB a widely accepted currency by global partners. Moreover, only with the internationalization of RMB can China form an independent global supply chain and use its own currency to support cross-border trade and investment.

The first chapter of this book analyzes the macroeconomic impact of foreign exchange intervention based on empirical studies that cover 26 economies. It discusses why most countries favor a floating exchange rate regime under the existing international monetary system. Sustained large-scale intervention in the foreign exchange market not only incurs direct costs but also hasunintended macroeconomic consequences on domestic prices, real interest rates, and asset prices. In fact, foreign exchange intervention has little effect in curbing capital outflow, but instead impedes the development of a risk management market and the internationalization of the RMB. The experiences from three major exchange rate policy adjustments in China that took place in 1994, 2005, and 2015also suggest that equilibrium exchange rates must be determined by market forces rather than subjective judgments.

The second chapter discusses the macroeconomic and microeconomic conditions that would facilitate a successful transition to a floating exchange rate. It evaluates China's macroeconomic soundness systematically using two sets of indicators: macroeconomic vulnerability assessment and systematic risk assessment. The term "free-floating" may be falsely associated with a loose and unregulated policy environment, but in fact any country with a successful floating exchange rate regime must adhere to rules-based and highly self-disciplined macroeconomic management. The key to successful macroeconomic management includes disciplined money supply, sustainable public debt, and well-managed external debt. In the absence of major micro- or macroeconomic imbalances, a country should strive to overcome the "fear of floating" and allowits exchange rate to float.

The third chapter discusses the importance of further developing the foreign exchange (FX) derivatives market in China. Although China has made some progress in developing its FX derivatives market in recent years, an underdeveloped over-the-counter (OTC) market without a futures market hasmeant that the FX derivatives market remains a weakness that is hindering the transition to a free-floating exchange rate regime. Compared with the OTC market, the FX futures markets can better meet the hedging needs of small and medium-sized enterprises (SMEs) due to its standardized products, greater transparency, stronger supervision, lower cost, and credit risk. Our empirical analysis on emerging countries also shows that FX futures can serve as a "stabilizer" and an important complement to the spot and OTC markets. Prudential regulation is essential to ensuring the stability of the FX derivatives market. Near-term priorities include gradually phasing out the current requirement of underlying exposures and allowing for a more market-based approach to risk management.

The fourth chapter explores the paths toward further opening up of the capital market and further internationalization of the RMB under a floating exchange rate. Considering the sheer size of the Chinese economy, the internationalization of the RMB and the openness of China's capital market lag behind its economic development. Therefore, it is crucial for China to expedite the creation of the conditions necessary for the adoption of a floating exchange rate regime so that the internationalization of the RMB can keep up with the growth and opening up of the Chinese economy. A floating exchange rate, a well-developed FX derivatives market, and a well-managed money supply and external debt would put China in a position to further open up its capital market with support from additional policy measures, such as further development of its bond and stock futures market.

In sum, this book demonstrates that, although foreign exchange intervention may appear to be "stability-enhancing", it does so at the expense of distortions to domestic macroeconomic variables. We argue that, with greater external pressures, the advantages of a flexible exchange rate will become all the more prominent. In the face of an especially complicated international environment, the choice of an exchange rate regime is no longer a "good or bad" issue, but a "life-or-death" issue. Moving toward a floating exchange rate is a logical choice for China and can lay the foundation for the further internationalization of the RMB. Such internationalization is not a peripheral issue that can be sacrificed, but a central issue that would determine whether the Chinese economy can stay resilient against external shocks without having to resort to closed-door policies.

This book reflects the authors' observation of and thinking over exchange rate policy issues and the RMB's internationalization in their decades-long work experiences. Many ideas presented herein are drawn from practical working experiences and real case scenarios, both in China and abroad, and are further examined by way of systematic analyses and empirical tests. The authors are grateful for the numerous discussions with experts in China and abroad who have contributed greatly to the writing of this book. We hope that the book will present readers with some new perspectives on China's exchange rate policy issues and RMB internationalization while also serving to motivate further research. Finally, the views presented in this book are solely those of the authors and do not represent the views of their associated institutions.

1 The Macroeconomic Impact of Foreign Exchange Intervention

Cross-Country Empirical Studies

The Macroeconomic Impact of Foreign Exchange Intervention: Background and Methodology

Mainstream views regarding the optimal choice of exchange rate policies have evolved over time, and the issue is still a matter of significant debate. In the early 1990s, a fixed exchange rate (pegged to the US dollar or German mark) was a popular option for developing countries, especially those transitioning toward market economies. However, the capital account crises and exchange rate collapse that took place in the late 1990s revealed the vulnerability of a fixed exchange rate and resulted in the wide perception that simple pegs might be too risky and that a country should either adopt a hard peg via monetary unions or currency boards, or use a free-floating exchange rate without government intervention (Ghosh and Ostry, 2009).

The collapse of the Argentine peso in 2002 once again shifted mainstream views with regard to the optimal choice of an exchange rate regime by raising new doubts about the viability of hard pegs. Discussions about the merits of an intermediate exchange rate regime followed suit. Yi and Tang (2001) proposed an expanded version of the "impossible trinity" and showed that a country does not have to fully give up any one of the trinity conditions (i.e., a fixed exchange rate, free capital mobility, or monetary independence). The authors argued that it is possible to achieve a combination of the three conditions proportionately. Their proposal suggested that an exchange rate regime does not necessarily have to be a clean float or a hard peg, but in practice, can be an intermediate regime that lies in between the two.

Husain et al. (2005) found that exchange rate regimes across countries have not exhibited an obvious tendency to evolve toward either a clean float or a hard peg. Instead, intermediate regimes have demonstrated greater sustainability over time. They also found that

DOI: 10.4324/9781003305668-1

the merits of a free-floating regime tend to become more prominent as an economy matures. In the early stage of economic development, a fixed exchange rate has the benefit of serving as a nominal anchor that keeps inflation in check. However, as an economy matures and its policy credibility improves, the price-stabilizing function of a fixed exchange rate becomes less important. A free-floating regime, on the other hand, appears more beneficial as mature economies with a free-floating exchange rate tend to achieve superior economic performance. The 2009 International Monetary Fund (IMF) review of exchange rate regimes similarly pointed out that the appropriate choice of exchange rate regime should depend on country-specific contexts: A rigid exchange rate regime helps anchor inflation expectations and sustain economic output, but simultaneously puts greater constraints on macroeconomic policies, increases vulnerability to crises, and impedes macroeconomic adjustments against external shocks (Ostry and Ghosh, 2009).

More recently, especially since the global financial crisis and the subsequent massive scale of unconventional monetary easing, economies have increased the use of capital controls and foreign exchange intervention (FXI) to manage the heightened volatility of exchange rates and capital flows. Some studies have provided a theoretical justification for the use of sterilized FXI, even for economies that adopt inflation-targeting (IT) regimes (Alla et al., 2017; Benes et al., 2013; Cavallino, 2019; Ostry et al., 2015). Another large body of empirical studies has analyzed the effectiveness of FXI in stabilizing the exchange rate (e.g., Adler et al., 2015; Blanchard et al., 2016; Daude et al., 2014; Fratzscher et al., 2015).

Despite the potential merits of using FXI,[1] most studies do recognize that FXI is not a free lunch and should be used only under very rare circumstances. Recent literature, however, has paid less attention to the potential costs associated with FXI.[2] Although China has significantly reduced its intervention in the foreign exchange market in recent years, understanding the macroeconomic consequences of FXI remains important so as to gain insights that may help with China's macroeconomic management.

We set out to investigate both the effectiveness and potential consequences of FXI by drawing from international experiences and a China-specific context. Based on vector autoregression (VAR) analyses across 26 countries, we show that while FXI is effective in mitigating nominal exchange rate fluctuations in the short run, its impact on the real exchange rate is less significant. Our results suggest that while FXI can limit adjustments of the nominal exchange rate, it simultaneously induces the real exchange rate to adjust through domestic prices, which may not be conducive to countering the impact of external shocks. Specifically, we find that in the face of external financial shocks, countries with more intensive use of FXI experience greater general and asset price volatility. We further examine China's macroeconomic responses to external shocks over the past decades and find that they were broadly consistent with the international experiences of intervening countries.

The simple methodological framework adopted in this chapter is meant to examine a broad set of macroeconomic variables and has limitations. We hope that our findings serve to motivate more structural analysis on FXI's macroeconomic impact in the future.

Empirical methodology: A key challenge in estimating the macroeconomic impact of FXI arises from the endogenous nature of FXI: FXI is often triggered by contemporaneous changes in macroeconomic variables, such as the exchange rate, yet the implementation of FXI will in turn affect the same macroeconomic variables, making it difficult to identify the causal impact from FXI. Many studies have resorted to the use of either instrumental variables to identify the exogenous variations in FXI, or the use of high-frequency data and event-study techniques to resolve reverse causality. We adopt a methodology similar to that in Blanchard et al. (2015), which constructs a capital flow measure deemed exogenous from the perspective of individual economies, and study whether exchange rates in countries with or without FXI exhibit different responses to the capital flow measure. We apply the methodology to investigate the impulse response of additional macroeconomic variables to FXI and compare the findings to a case study in the context of China.[3] Our reduced-form VAR is meant to capture how countries with varying degrees of FXI differ in their macroeconomic responses broadly; further research can deploy more robust structural vector autoregression (SVAR) to investigate the underlying transmission mechanisms.

The empirical results suggest that in the face of external shocks, FXI can mitigate nominal exchange rate fluctuations, but it has limited impact on the real exchange rate. Moreover, in the face of external shocks, countries with FXI experience greater general and asset price volatility compared to countries with a free-floating exchange rate. The results also suggest that although FXI may be effective in stabilizing the nominal exchange rate, the real exchange rate may achieve self-adjustments through domestic prices, but painful domestic consequences are likely in the course of adjustment. We find that the macroeconomic responses to external shocks in China were broadly consistent with the international experiences of intervening countries.

To investigate the macroeconomic impact of FXI, we conduct VAR analysis for a group of 26 countries individually. Like Blanchard et al. (2016),we classify the countries into two groups – namely, interveners and floaters – based on individual FXI responses to external financial shocks, or the "VIX" in our case.[4] Hence, the exogenous shock used in our model may also be considered a global financial shock. Half of our sample countries are grouped as interveners, while the other half, floaters. We use monthly data from 1990 to 2019 in our estimation.[5] The country-specific model takes the following form:

$$\left(I - A_l L - \ldots - A_p L^p\right) \cdot Y_{j,t} = \epsilon_{j,t}.$$

Specifically, L^p represents a lag operator of order p, $A_l \ldots A_p$ are 6×6 parameter matrices, and $Y_{j,t}$ represents the vector of exogenous and endogenous variables, defined as the following in the baseline specification:

$$Y_{j,t} \equiv \left[ER_{j,t} \ FXI_{j,t} F_{j,t} \ STOCK_{j,t} T_{j,t} VIX_{j,t} \right].$$

Specifically, $ER_{j,t}$ denotes changes in the nominal exchange rate vis-à-vis the US dollar. $F_{j,t}$ is the inflation indicator, measured by the average growth of the consumer price index (CPI) and producer price index (PPI). Throughout our estimations, we measure inflation as the average growth of CPI and PPI to capture the price responses in both the consumer and the producer sector.[6] $STOCK_{j,t}$ indicates the change in the stock market index, and $T_{j,t}$ denotes short-term interest differentials vis-à-vis the US, which is meant to control for contemporaneous changes in monetary policy stance (unsterilized FXI). Lastly, $VIX_{j,t}$ denotes changes in the S&P 500 volatility index, which captures global financial conditions and serves as the exogenous variable in our model. We include additional variables, such as real exchange rate and real interest rate, in subsequent estimations of the model.[7] For comparability, we use bilateral real exchange rate (vis-à-vis the US dollar) as our real exchange rate variable. We also conduct robustness checks using real effective exchange rates (REER).

$FXI_{j,t}$ indicates FXI, which is measured by changes in the stock of foreign reserves (normalized by quarterly gross domestic product (GDP)) in the benchmark specification.[8] An advantage of measuring FXI using changes in the stock of foreign reserves is that such a proxy is consistently available across countries and typically spans a long period, that is, 1990–2019 in our baseline specification. But a disadvantage of such a proxy is that it is polluted by valuation changes and investment income flows, and it includes central bank operations vis-à-vis residents and non-residents, which affect the level of foreign reserves but do not constitute FXI. To address this concern, we reestimate the baseline model and subsequent empirical tests using an alternative novel database of FXI (Adler et al., 2021) as a robustness check. The novel database compiles officially published and proxied FXI in both the spot and derivatives markets, covering the period from 2000 to 2020. For brevity, we report the estimation results using the simple measure in the main text while leaving the estimation results using the novel database in the Appendix. The estimates show that both measures of FXI yield similar conclusions.

The baseline model is used to group our sample countries into interveners and floaters by estimating country-specific FXI responses to external shocks. We classify the countries based on the rankings of their cumulative FXI responses at a specified time horizon. Such a classification methodology is based solely on the statistically estimated FXI responses to external financial shocks. Some countries grouped as floaters might intervene strongly in the foreign exchange market, albeit in response to other types of shocks, and are therefore not reflected in our estimation.

The data for nominal exchange rates and foreign reserves are from the IMF's International Financial Statistics (IFS). Data for inflation, interest rates, and stock market index are from Haver Analytics. Data for the "VIX" are from the Chicago Board Options Exchange.

Cross-Country Empirical Findings

FXI Responses and the Nominal Exchange Rate

Figure 1.1 depicts the cumulative impulse responses of FXI to an external financial shock at t = 6. The external financial shock in all our reported results refers to a standard deviation increase in our exogenous variable (i.e., changes in the "VIX") and can be interpreted as a worsening of external financial conditions. The y-axis indicates percentage changes. The significant cross-sectional variations in FXI responses provide the basis for us to construct a *de-facto FXI regime classification* (Table 1.1) based on the rankings of their responses (i.e., whether their cumulative responses are smaller or larger than the median).

Our focus is on the cross-section of impulse response functions of the domestic variables to the exogenous variable. We start by estimating the country-by-country impulse response functions using the above VAR

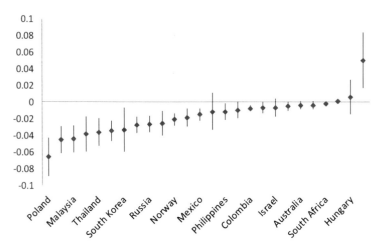

Figure 1.1 Cumulative responses of FXI to an external shock.

Note: Cumulative impulse responses from individually estimated VAR models, at t = 6. One standard deviation bands are reported.

Table 1.1 Categorization of de facto exchange rate regimes

De Facto Exchange Rate Regimes			
Interveners		*Floaters*	
Bolivia	Poland	Australia	Indonesia
India	Romania	Brazil	Israel
Malaysia	Russia	Canada	Philippines
Mexico	South Korea	Chile	South Africa
New Zealand	Thailand	Colombia	Sri Lanka
Norway	Turkey	Czech Republic	Sweden
Peru		Hungary	

Sources: Blanchard et al. (2015) and authors' calculation.

model. We then take the weighted average of country estimates for the group of floaters and group of interveners, respectively,[9] and compare the impulse response functions of key variables across the two groups.

Figure 1.2a depicts the impulse response functions of changes in foreign reserves to a one standard deviation shock to the exogenous variable. The solid lines represent the weighted average of individual impulse response functions for the two country groups. The dashed lines represent the associated confidence bands. The results show that foreign reserves among interveners (versus floaters) experience a larger decline in response to an external shock. The difference is significant, both economically and statistically.

Figure 1.2b depicts the impulse response functions of the average nominal exchange rate to an exogenous shock. A positive value indicates a depreciation vis-à-vis the US dollar. The results show that the nominal exchange rates of floaters experience a larger depreciation than those of the interveners in response to an external shock.[10] Again, the difference is economically and statistically significant. The empirical results are broadly consistent with those of Blanchard et al. (2015).

The results in Figure 1.1 suggest that FXI is effective in mitigating the nominal exchange rate fluctuations in the face of an external financial shock. Estimation results using the alternative novel FXI database yield similar results.

Responses of the Real Exchange Rate

Figure 1.3 compares the impulse response functions of real exchange rates between the two groups of countries. Although the extent of depreciation remains different across the two groups and is still larger for the floaters, they become economically smaller and statistically less significant (versus Figure 1.2b). The results suggest that FXI is less effective in stabilizing the bilateral real exchange rate (versus the nominal exchange rate) in the face of an external shock. The result is robust to alternative measures of FXI. We also conduct a robustness check using REER, and the findings in Figure 1.3 still hold.

The results in Figure 1.3 suggest that real exchange rates among interveners can still adjust despite the presence of FXI, which limits nominal exchange rate flexibility, but such external adjustments are likely to be less desirable than those of the floaters for the following reasons. First, real exchange rate adjustments through falling domestic prices can be painful as they amplify the deflationary pressure that may result from external shocks. Second, real exchange rate depreciation by way of falling domestic prices may not fully release depreciation pressure due to potential downward price rigidities: Domestic prices may not adjust flexibly in response to external shocks. As Figure 1.3 shows, real exchange rates depreciate to a lesser extent among interveners (vs. floaters) in response to the external shock.

Figure 1.4a further compares the impulse response functions of the nominal exchange rate and the real exchange rate among the group of interveners. Real exchange rates experience greater depreciation than nominal exchange rates in response to an external shock, suggesting that

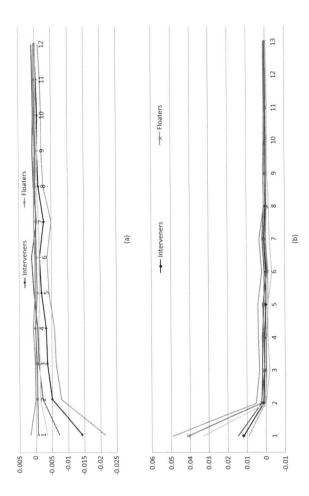

Figure 1.2 Responses of foreign reserves and exchange rates to an external shock. (a) FXI IRF: interveners versus floaters.
(b) Nominal exchange rate IRF: interveners versus floaters.

Note: The figures depict impulse response functions to a one standard deviation shock to the exogenous variable. Solid and dashed lines represent the weighted average of impulse responses and their (60%) confidence bands respectively, with weights that are inversely proportional to the standard deviation of each impulse response. The x-axis indicates number of months, while the y-axis indicates percentage changes.

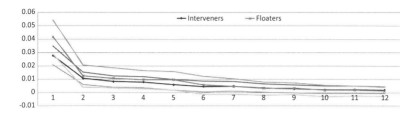

Figure 1.3 Responses of real exchange rates.

FXI could keep the nominal exchange rate stable, but the real exchange rate could still adjust by way of falling domestic prices. One possible interpretation of the observation is that FXI, in practice, may not always be fully sterilized, especially in the short run, thereby resulting in a change of monetary stance that may affect relative prices. Another possibility is that external financial shocks are contractionary in nature and may cause deflationary pressure domestically, and limitations on exchange rate flexibility impede external adjustments that would counter the deflationary pressure of the shock.

In contrast, Figure 1.4b shows that for the group of floaters, nominal and real exchange rates exhibit relatively similar responses to external shocks, suggesting that external shocks among floaters are not accompanied by significant changes in relative prices. One way to interpret such an observation is that nominal exchange rate depreciation helps facilitate external adjustments and serves to counter the deflationary pressure that may result from the external shock.

Figure 1.4a suggests that, although FXI may stabilize nominal exchange rates, real exchange rates may achieve adjustments through changes in relative prices. Figure 1.5 depicts the inflation[11] responses to external shocks for the two country groups. The results show that interveners experience greater deflationary pressure in the aftermath of an external shock, consistent with the findings in Figure 1.4a.

The impact of FXI on prices may also translate into an impact on the real interest rate. We test real interest rate responses to external shocks by adding a real interest rate variable to the baseline model. Figure 1.6 compares the average impulse response functions of real interest rates between floaters and interveners. The results show that in response to an external shock, average real interest rates among the floaters remain relatively unchanged but rise among the interveners. Rising real interest rates may amplify the impact of external shocks, aggravate the repayment burden of debtors, and further exacerbate domestic deflationary

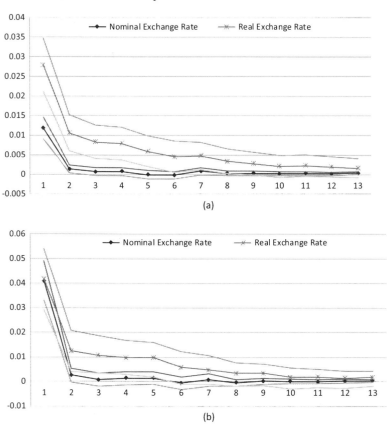

Figure 1.4 Comparing the responses of nominal and real exchange rates.
(a) Interveners IRF: nominal versus real exchange rate. (b) Floaters IRF: nominal versus real exchange rate.

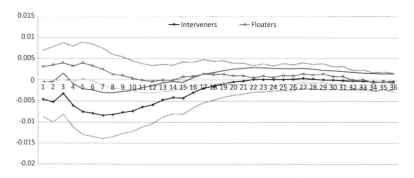

Figure 1.5 Responses of inflation.

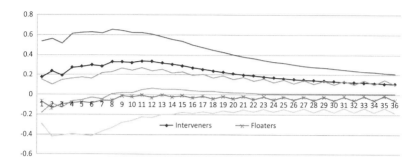

Figure 1.6 Response of real interest rates.

pressure. Although the differences across the two groups are not statistically significant, estimation results using alternative FXI measures similarly show that the average real interest rate among interveners rises persistently in response to external shocks.

Figure 1.7 compares the average impulse response functions of stock and housing prices to external shocks across the two country groups. The results show that stock prices generally fall in response to an external shock, consistent with findings in the global financial cycle (GFC) literature, but the average decline is larger among interveners. A robustness check using alternative FXI measures yields similar findings, which are both economically and statistically significant. The reactions of housing prices to external shocks are more mixed but also appear larger among interveners. Although FXI is often relied upon as a policy tool to reduce market volatility, we find no evidence that FXI can mitigate domestic asset price volatility.

Indeed, to the extent that FXI is effective in stabilizing the nominal exchange rate, it also constrains the role of the exchange rate as a "shock absorber", and may amplify the impact of external shocks on domestic asset prices. For instance, although FXI may mitigate nominal exchange rate depreciation in response to external shocks, it prevents depreciation expectations from being reflected in market prices in a timely manner and prolongs arbitrage opportunities, which may accelerate capital outflows and increase market volatility. Another possibility is that, to the extent that FXI contributes to rising real interest rates, as shown in Figure 1.6, it increases the opportunity costs of investing in the stock and housing markets, and may trigger downward pressure on stock and housing prices.

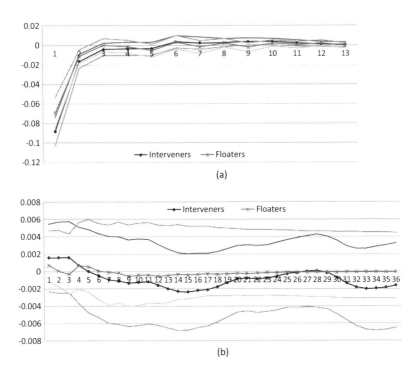

Figure 1.7 Response of asset prices. (a) Stock price IRF: floaters versus interveners. (b) Housing price IRF: floaters versus interveners.

Note: The figures depict impulse response functions to a one standard deviation shock to the exogenous variable. Solid and dashed lines represent the weighted average of impulse responses and their (60%) confidence bands respectively, with weights that are inversely proportional to the standard deviation of each impulse response. The x-axis indicates number of months, while the y-axis indicates percentage changes.

Of course, asset price dynamics are inherently complicated and can be driven by many other factors. Further research is needed to investigate the precise role of FXI in influencing asset prices. The upshot is that we find no evidence that FXI can mitigate asset price volatility. On the contrary, our results suggest that FXI may actually cause greater asset price volatility.

Transmission of FXI: The empirical results presented herein show that differences in macroeconomic responses to external shocks exist between the two groups, suggesting that FXI can potentially generate macroeconomic impacts. We briefly discuss and review the transmission of FXI from a theoretical perspective.

FXI can generate macroeconomic impact via many channels. FXI that is not fully sterilized entails a change in monetary stance and can subsequently affect exchange rate and domestic prices. FXI aimed at countering depreciation pressure, for instance, consists of selling foreign currencies and buying domestic currencies, which can be considered a reduction in the central bank's balance sheet. Without complete sterilization, the reduced balance sheet will result in a tightening of the money supply, contributing to deflationary pressure through falling general prices, rising real interest rates, and potentially falling asset prices.

Even with complete sterilization, FXI may still generate macroeconomic impact. The literature on the transmission mechanism of sterilized FXI is vast and rich, and most notably includes works on the portfolio balance channel. The portfolio balance channel (Henderson and Rogoff, 1982; Kouri, 1982; Branson and Henderson, 1985) is predicated primarily on imperfect substitutability between domestic and foreign assets so that any changes in asset composition could affect risk premia. Recent works have advanced the portfolio balance theory using microfounded frameworks to model the underlying financial friction (Gabaix and Maggiori, 2015; Chang and Velasco, 2017; Cavallino, 2019; Fanelli and Straub, 2020). Sterilized FXI may also generate macroeconomic impact via the signaling channel by revealing the central bank's policy intentions, thereby influencing market expectations.[12]

Direct Costs of FXI

The empirical results presented herein suggest that while interveners experience less nominal exchange rate volatility in response to external shocks, they bear the consequence of additional adjustments in domestic general and asset prices. Such macroeconomic consequences can be costly but may be overlooked or underestimated as they may not be directly observable.

FXI can also incur more direct costs, including the buildup of external imbalances, loss of foreign reserves, suppression of external investment returns, underdevelopment of the foreign exchange market, and conflicting goals between monetary policy and exchange rate policy, which we will briefly discuss next.

FXI may impede timely adjustments of the balance of payments in response to negative external shocks. FXI that attempts to counter depreciation pressure can slow the adjustments of the balance of payments. The IMF's External Balance Assessment (EBA) conducted an empirical analysis and found that FXI results in a buildup of external imbalances, especially in countries with capital account restrictions (Phillips et al., 2013).[13]

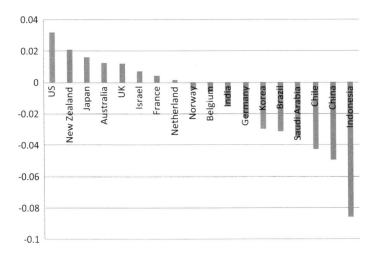

Figure 1.8 Cross-country average net external investment returns (2000–2018).
Source: Das et al. (2020).

Note: Das et al. (2020) estimate external investment returns using the IMF's cross-border investment stock and flow data, see Gourinchas and Rey (2007) for more details regarding the methodology.

FXI could also accelerate the depletion of foreign reserves. Figure 1.2a shows that in the face of external shocks, interveners suffer a much larger decline in foreign reserves compared to floaters, with a difference in FXI of close to 1.5% of quarterly GDP.

FXI also incurs quasi-fiscal costs that may arise from the economic opportunity costs of holding reserve assets. Sustained FXI could inculcate a long-term dependence on reserve accumulation, a large portion of which is typically invested in low-return asset classes such as sovereign bonds, suppressing the net external investment returns of a country. Adler and Mano (2016) introduced a measurement for the marginal and total costs associated with foreign reserve accumulation and showed that the fiscal costs of sustained FX intervention are non-negligible across a large set of countries. Moreover, reserve accumulation crowds out the private sector's external investment, which could hamper the efficient allocation of outbound capital. Figure 1.8 shows that China's average net external returns from 2000 to 2018 lay in the negative region,[14] lagging behind many other emerging market economies.

FXI can also inhibit the development of foreign exchange derivatives markets. FXI, in practice, may not always involve direct purchases and sales in the spot market, but may alternatively take place in the derivatives markets with policy measures such as requiring payment of foreign exchange risk reserves. Intervention in the derivatives market serves the purpose of countering depreciation or appreciation pressure without directly tapping foreign reserve assets. An important side effect of FXI in the derivatives market is that the distorted price or additional cost of hedging as a result of intervention policies may drive away investors who have real hedging needs, thereby creating market barriers to risk-management tools. Such intervention policies contradict a sustainable market-based approach to risk management and can result in underdevelopment of the derivatives market. Hofman et al. (2020) found that the case for FXI appears strongest in countries with severe currency mismatch and underdeveloped markets. Their findings suggest that sustained use of FXI may entrench adverse initial conditions such as an underdeveloped market, giving rise to a negative policy-induced feedback loop.

Another costly consequence of FXI is that it can put the central bank in a dilemma by creating conflicting goals between inflation and exchange rate targets. An important mandate of the central bank is to maintain price stability, but inflation targets may be compromised if the central bank simultaneously attempts to achieve an exchange rate target. Granted, there are circumstances under which inflation targets are compatible with exchange rate targets. For example, when a country tries to combat deflationary pressure, FXI that sells domestic currencies in exchange for foreign currencies helps ramp up inflation. Similarly, when a country experiences inflationary pressure, FXI that sells foreign currencies in exchange for domestic currencies helps rein in inflation. However, under many circumstances in practice, the objectives of FXI often conflict with inflation targets. For instance, countries often resort to FXI under a crisis scenario with a rising current account deficit, capital outflows, exchange rate depreciation, and deflation. FXI that involves reserve sales may reinforce deflationary pressure if no immediate and complete sterilization policies are in place. On the other hand, reserve accumulation typically takes place under a rising current account surplus, capital inflows, appreciation pressure, and inflation. Hence, FXI that is not fully sterilized could further fuel inflation.

China Case Study and Conclusion

We use the VAR model to study the impulse responses of China's macroeconomic variables to external shocks. As with the cross-country

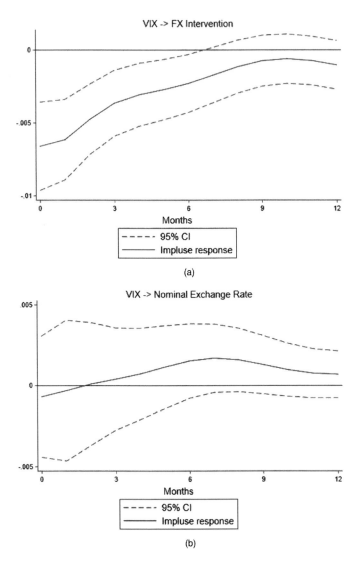

Figure 1.9 Response of FXI and nominal exchange rate to external shocks.
(a) China: FXI IRF. (b) China: nominal exchange rate IRF.

analysis, we estimate the model with monthly data from 1990 to 2018.[15] Our results suggest that China's macroeconomic responses to external shocks are broadly consistent with international experiences among interveners.

Figure 1.9a depicts FXI's impulse response function to an external shock. The results show that over the past three decades, foreign reserves did fall in response to external shocks, indicating the presence of FXI in China during the period. Figure 1.9b depicts the impulse response function of the nominal exchange rate, which exhibits a lagged and relatively small depreciation in response to external shocks.

Figure 1.10a depicts the impulse response functions of the real exchange rate to external shocks. The result suggests that, although FXI in China limits nominal exchange rate adjustments in response to external shocks, it induces the real exchange rate to adjust through domestic prices: The real exchange rate depreciates quite significantly against external shocks. Adjustments to the real exchange rate, particularly by way of declining domestic prices, are unintended consequences of restricting the nominal exchange rate flexibility and can be costly to the macro-economy. Figure 1.10b confirms that external shocks induce deflationary pressure domestically, resembling the observations among interveners.

Figure 1.11 depicts the impulse response function of the real interest rate to external shocks. The real interest rate rises in response to external shocks, which could amplify the domestic impact of external shocks as it raises the real cost of borrowing and is contractionary in nature.

Figure 1.12 depicts the impulse response functions of stock and housing prices to external shocks. Consistent with international experience, stock and housing prices in China fall in response to external shocks, with a magnitude that is closer to that of the interveners (Figure 1.7a).

These results show that, over the past three decades, external shocks to China were generally followed by FXI. Moreover, external shocks were accompanied by relatively mild nominal exchange rate fluctuations, deflationary pressure, real exchange rate depreciation, rising real interest rates, and falling asset prices, similar to the experiences of other interveners.

However, the estimated responses to external shocks are only empirically associated with FXI. We have yet to examine whether FXI has any causal relationship with the relevant macroeconomic variables. To this end, Table 1.2 depicts a Granger causality test that includes our variables of interest. The results show that FXI can Granger-cause real exchange rate, general prices, the real interest rate, and asset prices. Drawing from our cross-country empirical evidence, our results suggest that FXI is likely a contributing factor to China's exhibited macroeconomic adjustments in response to external shocks.

Can foreign exchange intervention stem capital outflows? FXI is often used as a policy instrument to counter capital outflow pressure when

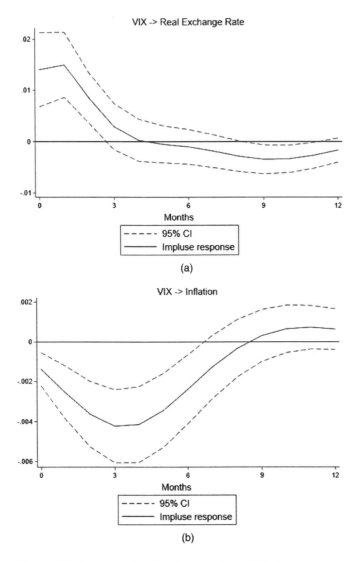

Figure 1.10 Response of real exchange rate and inflation rate to an external shock. (a) China: real exchange rate IRF. (b) China: inflation IRF.

market volatility heightens, but the effectiveness of such policy measures remains a matter of significant debate. We conduct a VAR analysis with three endogenous variables (i.e., net capital outflows, US–China interest rate differentials, and changes in foreign reserves) and an exogenous

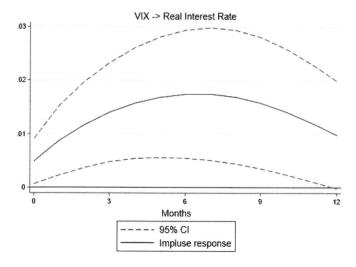

Figure 1.11 Response of the real interest rate to external shocks.

variable (i.e., changes in the "VIX") to investigate the impact of FXI on capital outflows. Table 1.3 depicts the Granger causality test among the endogenous variables. The results show that FXI can Granger-cause net capital flows. However, rather than stemming capital outflows, capital outflows respond positively to FXI after the external shock hits (Figure 1.13), suggesting that FXI may have actually accelerated capital outflows. In sum, we find no evidence that FXI has helped stem capital outflows in China over the sample period.

Our results suggest that, over the past three decades, FXI in China has played a role in smoothing out nominal exchange rate fluctuations against external financial shocks, which may have helped alleviate market panic to a certain extent when volatility heightened. Yet it may have simultaneously caused unintended domestic macroeconomic consequences that could impair adjustments against external shocks. For example, the fact that the real exchange rate adjusts more flexibly than the nominal exchange rate suggests that limitations on the nominal exchange rate may induce greater general and asset price volatility domestically in response to external shocks. The macroeconomic consequences of FXI in China are broadly consistent with those in other countries that use FXI actively.

Sterilization policies themselves are not without costs. Our estimations controlled for the central bank's sterilization policies, without which the

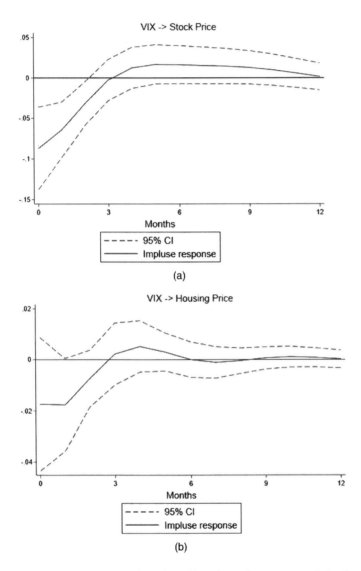

Figure 1.12 Response of stock and housing prices to external shocks.
(a) China: stock price IRF. (b) China: housing price IRF.

impact of FXI could be even stronger. If the central bank sterilizes by issuing central bank notes, it has to bear the interest rate charges on the central bank notes. If the central bank raises the reserve requirement ratio, the cost is effectively passed on to commercial banks, which

Table 1.2 FXI's impact in China: Granger causality test

Grander causality Wald tests

Equation	Excluded	chi²	df	Prob>chi²
ER	FXI	5.751	2	0.056
F	FXI	11.24	2	0.004
STOCK	FXI	5.541	2	0.063
rir	FXI	7.423	2	0.024
T	FXI	0.0118	2	0.994

Note: ER, FXI, F, STOCK, rir, and T correspond to the variables for exchange rate, FXI, inflation, asset price changes, real interest rate, and short-term interest differentials.

Table 1.3 FXI's impact on China's capital flows: Granger causality test

Granger causality Wald tests

Equation	Excluded	chi²	df	Prob>chi²
Capital flow net	FXI	6.618	2	0.037
Capital flow net	T	3.446	2	0.179
FXI	Capital flow net	23.09	2	0
FXI	T	13.73	2	0.001
T	Capital flow net	0.27	2	0.874
T	FXI	1.768	2	0.413

Note: Capital flow net, FXI, and T correspond to the variables for net capital outflows, FXI, and short-term interest rate differentials.

may in turn increase the cost of lending to borrowers. If the commercial banks respond to the higher reserve requirement ratio by shifting businesses off their balance sheets or to the non-bank sector, they will create shadow banking businesses and increase financial stability risks. Further research is needed to empirically confirm the identified transmission channels of sterilization policies.

In sum, based on cross-country VAR analyses, we find that, although FXI is effective in mitigating nominal exchange rate fluctuations, it has limited impact on the real exchange rate. We find that real exchange rates among intervening countries adjust more flexibly than nominal exchange rates do, suggesting that the stability of the nominal exchange rate may be achieved at the expense of greater domestic volatility. Both our cross-country analysis and a representative single-country case analysis show that in the face of external financial shocks, FXI may result in greater general and asset price volatility, which are unintended domestic consequences. China's macroeconomic responses to external shocks

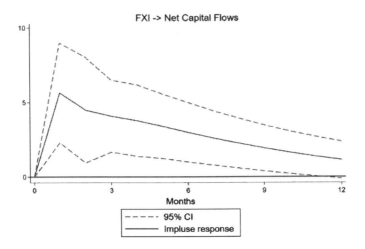

Figure 1.13 FXI's impact on China's capital flows.

over the past three decades are broadly consistent with international experiences among intervening countries. The reduced-form VAR used in this chapter has methodological limitations; future research could examine the macroeconomic transmissions of FXI more structurally. Considering that the balance of payments is one of the most critical macroeconomic equilibrium relationships, there are reasons to believe that the costs of external imbalances may have been underestimated in intervening countries. A flexible exchange rate is critical in cushioning external shocks without causing unintended and potentially costly domestic consequences. Greater exchange rate flexibility can also help prevent conflicting monetary policy goals and enhance central bank credibility, which are important in ensuring greater independence in designing and implementing domestic macroeconomic policies.

The Significance of Exchange Rate Flexibility in the Context of the Three Exchange Rate Policy Adjustments in China and Three Crises

Exchange rate reflects the relative price of two currencies, and serves as an adapter that connects China and the world. It affects almost all internal and external economic indicators. The empirical results presented in the previous chapter reveal that FXI limits the role of exchange rate as an economic stabilizer, and exacerbates internal and external economic imbalances. In this chapter, we conduct a historical review and look at the empirical results through the lens of the last three exchange rate policy adjustments (1994, 2005, and 2015) and crises (1997, 2008, and 2015). The review suggests that sustained and large-scale FXI will significantly distort domestic goods prices, real interest rates, and asset prices, consistent with international experiences.

China's exchange rate formation mechanism has become increasingly market oriented over the last three decades. Past exchange rate reforms have advanced amid challenges, trials, and even setbacks, but significant progress has been made. Each reform has made the RMB exchange rate significantly more market oriented, reduced balance of payment (BOP) and domestic macroeconomic imbalances, and strengthened China's resilience against economic crises. Furthermore, reforming the exchange rate formation mechanism has effectively advanced China's opening up to the outside world.

Nonetheless, previous exchange rate reforms have been interrupted during economic crises, but there has been little research and exploration regarding the economic consequences of such interruptions. During the 1997 and 2008 financial crises, the trading band of the RMB exchange rate narrowed sharply, resulting in an interruption of both the 1994 and the 2005 exchange rate reforms. FXI and the strengthening of capital controls suppressed the stabilizing role of the exchange rate, and prevented the BOP from self-adjustments through exchange rate fluctuations, exacerbating the deflationary effect of the crises, and in turn, banks' non-performing loans (NPL) and a debt crisis.

The RMB was not devalued after the 1997 Asian financial crisis broke out, resulting in rising deflationary pressure and rapid accumulation of bad loans at banks, eventually forcing the government to carry out a large-scale capital injection into the commercial banks and the separation of non-performing loans in 1998 and 1999. During the 2005 exchange rate reform, the exchange rate regime was modified, but an immediate appreciation of the RMB did not take place. Instead, the currency took its time to appreciate against the backdrop of FXI, which caused the current account surplus to balloon. During the 2008 global financial crisis, the RMB did not depreciate sufficiently to counter falling external demand and rising capital outflow pressure. China therefore had to depend primarily on the State's RMB 4 trillion stimulus package to mitigate the impact of the crisis. It is worth noting that such fiscal measures significantly increased the fiscal and debt burden of both the central and local governments, causing non-negligible economic costs.

A similar economic imbalance occurred prior to the August 11, 2015, exchange rate reform. After the US Federal Reserve announced a tapering of its quantitative easing policy in the second half of 2013, global liquidity tightened abruptly. China's cross-border capital flows reversed, and expectations of the RMB's depreciation began to build quickly. Confronted with the pressure to depreciate, however, the RMB/USD exchange rate did not adjust promptly and adequately, and China had to again suffer economic consequences such as deflation. A historical review of the previous exchange rate reforms and their interruptions during economic crises is therefore necessary to more systematically examine the direct or indirect economic costs of an inflexible exchange rate.

A historical review of China's exchange rate regime. A floating rate system was implemented upon the founding of the People's Republic of China, but the lack of gold and silver as well as the Korean War resulted in significant exchange rate volatility. From 1953 to 1972, China adopted a single fixed exchange rate system. As the planned economic system gradually developed and improved, China's exchange rate remained generally stable for a long period of time. With the collapse of the Bretton Woods system in 1973, Western nations generally shifted to a floating exchange rate system. China adopted a single floating exchange rate system based on a basket of currencies, and the RMB entered an appreciation cycle that lasted until about 1980.

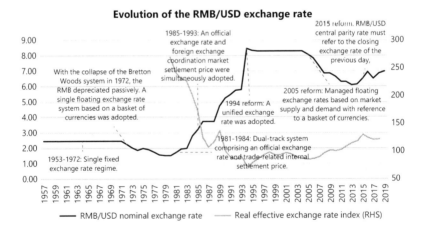

Figure 1.14 Evolution of the RMB/USD exchange rate.

Source: International Monetary Fund (IMF) and Bank of International Settlements (BIS).

To encourage exports among foreign trade enterprises, China implemented a dual-track exchange rate system from 1981 to 1984 comprising an official exchange rate and a trade-related internal settlement price, and an FX retention system for foreign trade enterprises was introduced. Under the FX retention system, foreign trade enterprises were required to sell all their foreign currencies to a government-designated bank at the official rate while obtaining a certificate based on the portion retained by the enterprise, that is, an FX quota. When an enterprise was in need of FX, it would approach a bank with the FX certificate to purchase FX based on the internal FX settlement price. The existence of different FX prices led to rapid growth in over-the-counter (OTC) trading. Many enterprises with a quota would withdraw FX at the official price and earn the spread at the OTC market. The dual-track FX system during this period led to rampant speculation, resulting in regulatory challenges in the FX market. Meanwhile, losses in the core businesses of some foreign trade enterprises continued to widen as they sought to profit from arbitrage opportunities in the FX market, and business enthusiasm among non-trade enterprises was dampened.

Between 1985 and 1993, the dual-track system shifted to the adoption of an official exchange rate and FX coordination market settlement price, but it could no longer meet China's economic development needs. In 1988, China liberalized the FX coordination market rate, which began to float freely according to market supply and demand. The proportion of transactions using the FX coordination market rate continued to expand: by the end of 1993, it accounted for 85% of the country's import-export FX turnover. As the Chinese economy continued to open up and its market-oriented reforms continued to deepen, the dual-track exchange rate system could no longer support evolving market needs. With an overheated economy, overvalued official exchange rate, growing trade surplus, and mounting devaluation pressure, the State Council introduced a key exchange rate reform in early 1994.

Prior to the exchange rate reform in 1994, significant macroeconomic imbalances had built up in China. China posted a relatively large trade surplus of USD 11.6 billion in 1993, with foreign reserves of just USD 21.2 billion. The significantly higher FX coordination market rate vis-à-vis the official rate reflected the overvaluation of the official rate, resulting in excessive export demand. Meanwhile, money supply was growing too quickly, with both CPI and PPI increasing by 14.7% and 19.6%, respectively. Devaluation pressure of the official rate rose dramatically, while negative real interest rate accelerated capital outflows.

The 1994 exchange rate reform not only alleviated economic imbalances, but also developed the foundational framework of China's current exchange rate regime.[16] On January 1, 1994, the "dual" RMB exchange rates were unified. The 5.8 (USD/RMB) official rate was abolished, and the exchange rate was uniformly adjusted to the coordination market rate of 8.7 (USD/RMB). In theory, the equilibrium exchange rate should be somewhere between the official rate and the coordination market rate; the unified exchange rate at 8.7 (USD/RMB) had overshot. Not only was market expectation of a devaluation fully reflected, it even reversed to one of appreciation. On April 4, 1994, the interbank FX market (China Foreign Exchange Trading System, CFETS) commenced operations under the supervision of the People's Bank of China (PBOC), and a managed floating exchange rate regime was introduced. By the end of 1994, the currency did not depreciate, but instead appreciated to 8.5 (USD/RMB). With devaluation expectations reflected, capital outflow pressure eased, and foreign direct investment (FDI) increased from USD 27.5 billion in 1993 to USD 33.7 billion in 1994. In the same year, imports and exports grew by 11.3% and 31.9%, respectively, and the current account reversed from a deficit to a surplus of 1.2% of GDP. Foreign reserves increased from USD 21.2 billion at the end of 1993 to USD 51.6 billion in 1994. The 1994 exchange rate reform laid the foundational framework of China's current exchange rate regime, that is, a managed floating exchange rate regime based on market supply and demand with reference to a basket of currencies.

The events prior to and following the 1994 exchange rate reform indicate that exchange rate depreciation, and even overshooting, was effective in cushioning internal and external economic shocks. The events prior to and following the 1994 exchange rate reform showed that artificially maintaining a significantly overvalued exchange rate is unsustainable. The existence of a market-oriented foreign exchange coordination rate offers valuable insights that facilitated the unification of the "dual" exchange rates: Allowing the official exchange rate to fully devalue, and overshoot appropriately, would not result in economic instability; in fact, it helped improve the BOP, attract capital inflows, and reverse market expectation from one of devaluation to appreciation.

The 1997 Asian financial crisis reversed the appreciation trend of the RMB exchange rate into devaluation pressure. The Chinese government committed not to devalue the RMB exchange rate relative to the USD, fixing it at 8.3 (USD/RMB). A fixed exchange rate, together with foreign exchange management measures may have eased the pressure from panic-driven capital outflows, but have also impeded the macroeconomy from self-adjusting to the shocks, causing significant economic costs.

A fixed exchange rate caused the RMB to appreciate significantly against Asian currencies, adding to the burden of exporters. During the Asian financial crisis, China fixed its exchange rate relative to the USD, while most Asian countries devalued their currencies against the USD to varying degrees, causing the RMB to appreciate significantly against major Asian currencies. Sluggish external demand coupled with an appreciating RMB added to the burden of exporters, exacerbating the decline in exports. To alleviate the plight of exporters, the State adopted a series of supporting measures such as increasing export tax rebate rates, giving more subsidies to foreign trade enterprises, and extending more foreign trade loans. The government was in fact relying on fiscal policy to alleviate the burden of trade companies, instead of allowing exchange rate adjustments to smooth imports and exports.

Fixing the exchange rate against the backdrop of devaluation pressure added to deflationary pressure, as indicated by the PPI. Enterprises had to contend with insidiously rising real interest rates. With falling producer prices, unchanged nominal principal, and interest payment burden, enterprise earnings deteriorated dramatically, and loan quality declined, with a debt crisis emerging and systematic financial risks intensifying. Under a fixed exchange rate regime, deflation became the only conduit for easing the devaluation pressure on RMB's REER, and for mitigating the deterioration of the current account.

Between 1997 and 1998, both PPI and CPI inflation rates languished in the negative territory, resulting in stubbornly high real interest rates; the real economy and financing environment deteriorated. High real interest rates not only constrained the gradual recovery in bank lending, but also led to a rapid buildup of bad loans among existing loans. During this time, state-owned enterprises (SOEs) faced operational difficulties, widening losses, and massive layoffs. In 1997, the central government responded to the operational difficulties of SOEs with a range of reform measures including a "three-year turnaround plan for SOEs", "grasp the large and let go of the small", debt for equity swaps, and downsizing to increase efficiency. To curb the spread of systematic risks, the State, for the first time, intervened by injecting RMB 270 billions of capital into State-owned commercial banks, and established four major asset management companies in 1999 to take over approximately RMB 1.4 trillion worth of NPLs from banks. These interventions may have effectively eased systemic financial risks, but the associated policy price tag is significant, including substantially higher fiscal expenditure and debt burden, as well as a sharp increase in unemployment. Most people however, did not realize that such economic costs were related to China's exchange rate policy.

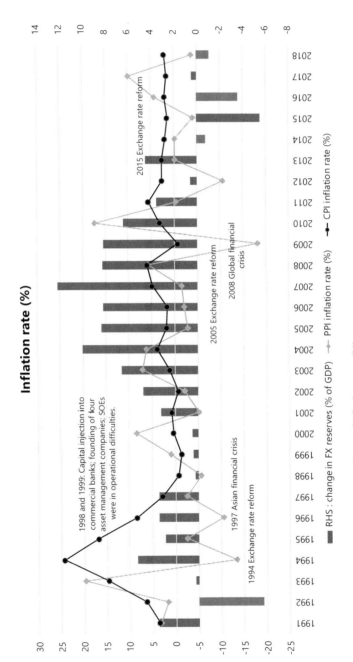

Figure 1.15 Macroeconomic impact of FXI: inflation rate (%).

Source: IMF, World Bank, and National Bureau of Statistics of China.

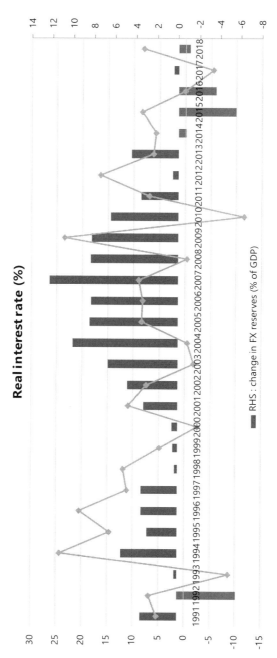

Figure 1.16 Macroeconomic impact of FXI: real interest rate (%).

Figure 1.17 Macroeconomic impact of FXI: current account balance (% of GDP).

Prior to the 2005 exchange rate policy adjustment, China's economic imbalances were mainly manifested in the form of continued surpluses in the current account and the capital and financial accounts. The RMB faced significant revaluation pressure. Between 2000 and 2005, China's current account surplus ballooned from USD 20 billion to USD 130 billion, the capital and financial account surplus leaped from USD 2 billion to USD 91.2 billion, and FDI rose from USD 40 billion to USD 60 billion. Meanwhile, foreign reserves increased from USD 165.5 billion to USD 818.8 billion.

The 2005 exchange rate policy adjustment reactivated the exchange rate that was frozen in 1998, and the RMB returned to a managed floating regime. On July 21, 2005, a new round of reforms to the RMB's exchange rate formation mechanism commenced. The reform mainly entailed abolishing the peg to the USD, and moving to a managed floating exchange rate regime based on market supply and demand, with reference to a basket of currencies. The USD/RMB exchange rate appreciated by 2.1%, from 8.28 to 8.11. The RMB central parity rate was now determined with reference to the closing rate of the previous day rather than to the weighted average interbank market rate in the previous day, but the daily trading band of ±0.3% for the RMB exchange rate remained unchanged. On January 4, 2006, the PBOC altered the central parity rate pricing system by further introducing a market maker system and a price inquiry trading mechanism.

A result of the 2005 exchange rate policy adjustment was the partial unwinding of the accumulation of economic imbalances. If the 1994 exchange rate reform could be described as a swift and complete adjustment of the exchange rate, the 2005 reform would be more of an incomplete adjustment. Following the 2005 reform, the RMB's unilateral revaluation pressure was only partially alleviated. The upward trend in the current account as well as capital and financial account surpluses decelerated. Inflation slowed somewhat, but appreciation and inflationary pressures remained. The central bank issued central bank bills and increased the reserve requirement ratio (RRR) as countermeasures against inflationary pressure. Sustained appreciation expectations continued to attract hot money inflows. The issuance of central bank bills and the RRR hike only partially offset the excessive growth in money supply that resulted from rising foreign reserves, which in turn led to a rapid increase in domestic prices, particularly asset prices.

During the 2008 financial crisis, the RMB's exchange rate fluctuations narrowed sharply, stalling the progress of exchange rate marketization that had taken place since 2005. Following the 2005 exchange rate reform, the RMB's exchange rate became more flexible and followed a steadily appreciating path, but equilibrium was never achieved. During the 2008 global financial crisis, the RMB was under temporary depreciation pressure, and RMB exchange rate fluctuations again narrowed significantly. From 2008 to mid-2010, the USD/RMB exchange rate generally stayed at the same level. It was not until June 19, 2010, that the PBOC again announced that it would increase the flexibility of the RMB exchange rate.

Inflexible exchange rates limited macroeconomic self-adjustments. When a currency fails to depreciate when it is supposed to, it usually leads to deflationary pressure. In the case of China, inflation rate reversed its rising trends and declined sharply. Real interest rates surged by more than 7% in 2008, adding to the financing cost of the corporate sector. The BOP was unable to adjust though the exchange rate, causing imports and exports to decline quickly. Deflationary pressure together with excessively high real interest rates intensified the downward pressure on growth and accelerated the buildup of financial risks, pushing the central government to introduce a large economic stimulus package later.

Although the economic stimulus package mitigated demand-side shocks, it significantly increased government and corporate leverage. Deflationary effect and downward pressure on growth resulted in the introduction of a large-scale government investment program. Given the restrictions on local government debt issuance, a large proportion of the investment projects were financed through local government financing platforms, leading to an increase in the hidden debt burden of local governments. Meanwhile, to circumvent financial supervision, many banks shifted relevant operations off their balance sheets, or shifted off-balance sheet items to non-bank financial institutions, sowing the seeds for shadow banking activities.

Prior to the 2015 exchange rate policy adjustments, economic imbalances reemerged in China as a result of inflexible exchange rates. On June 19, 2010, the PBOC announced that it would further advance the reform agenda for the exchange rate formation mechanism, and reiterated its intention to increase RMB exchange rate flexibility. From then on, the RMB embarked on a slow appreciation path. The PBOC later widened the USD/RMB trading band in the interbank spot foreign exchange market on April 16, 2012, and March 17, 2014, from 5% to 1% and 2%. The managed RMB exchange rate did not appreciate fully, and sustained revaluation expectation led to continued hot money inflows. To prevent the RMB exchange rate from appreciating too rapidly, the central bank intervened constantly by purchasing foreign exchange, which boosted foreign reserves and caused excessive growth in money supply as well as goods and asset prices. From mid-2010 to mid-2013, that is, prior to the Federal Reserve's announcement to "unwind" quantitative easing and the "taper tantrum" that ensued, the USD/RMB exchange rate appreciated from 6.81 to 6.17. During this period, China's producer prices and housing prices surged, foreign investment continued to flow in, and foreign reserves increased by about USD 1 trillion (see Figures 1.18, 1.19, 1.20, and 1.21).

In early 2014, foreign investment inflows reversed, and depreciation expectations started to form quickly, but the RMB exchange rate did not adjust promptly. Following the Federal Reserve's tapering announcement in 2013, the USD began to strengthen and global liquidity quickly tightened. Foreign investment inflows reversed, and expectations that the RMB would depreciate began to form, but the exchange rate again missed its window of opportunity to adjust promptly. Between early 2014 and the period prior to the August 11, 2015, exchange rate reform, the USD/RMB exchange rate remained stable between 6.1 and 6.2, and depreciation pressure began to build. Sustained depreciation pressure accelerated capital outflows. Meanwhile, the PBOC intervened in the FX market by selling FX, causing foreign reserves to decline. As a consequence, money supply tightened passively and producer prices declined sharply, while real interest rates surged; signs of deflation became increasingly apparent. In terms of asset prices, the stock market began its correction in July 2015 following a rally, and a market crash ensued. While the stock market collapse could be attributed to numerous

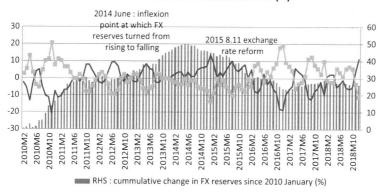

Figure 1.18 Macroeconomic impact of the August 11, 2015, exchange rate reform: PPI inflation rate and real interest rate (%).

Source: IMF, National Bureau of Statistics of China, Bloomberg, and CEIC.

Note: Real interest rate is defined as the difference between nominal lending rate and PPI inflation rate, and primarily reflects the financing cost of producers.

Capital flow indicators

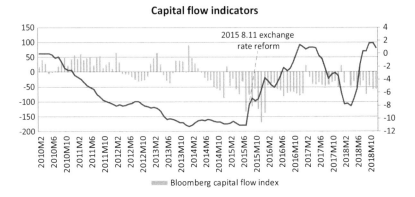

Figure 1.19 Macroeconomic impact of the August 11, 2015, exchange rate reform: capital flow indicators.

Stock market index

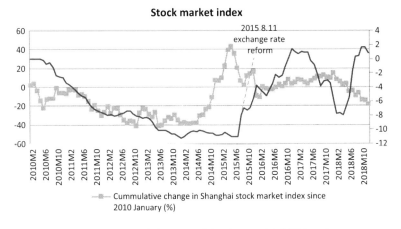

Figure 1.20 Macroeconomic impact of the August 11, 2015, exchange rate reform: stock market index.

reasons, including factors beyond exchange rate and monetary policies, the deflationary effect resulting from the inflexible exchange rate increased the probability of the crash. Meanwhile, residential property prices remained relatively stable thanks to a slowdown from earlier price appreciation.

A series of exchange rate policy adjustments that began in 2015 helped ease depreciation pressure on the RMB and mitigated economic imbalances. On August 11, 2015, the PBOC announced that it would adjust the USD/RMB central parity rate quotation mechanism. Market

Figure 1.21 Macroeconomic impact of the August 11, 2015, exchange rate reform: housing market index.

makers were required to refer to the closing exchange rate in the inter-bank FX market of the previous day, and provide the central parity rate to the China Foreign Exchange Trading Center (CFETC).[17] In February 2016, the central parity rate formation mechanism was specified, which improved the standardization, transparency, and marketization of the exchange rate system.[18] The one-off exchange rate adjustment (about 2%) on August 11, 2015, sparked a market correction, but the intensity of capital flow reversals and the extent to which the exchange rate was overvalued were underestimated. The adoption of the one-off incomplete adjustment, followed by defending the new level of exchange rate was incompatible with exchange rate overshooting principles, resulting in enormous depletion of foreign reserves. At the end of 2015, the PBOC adopted measures to guide a continued depreciation of the currency. The RMB depreciated gradually against the USD from 6.45 to 6.92 between end-2015 and end-2016. During the course of depreciation, FX management strengthened significantly, which suppressed FX outflows, and partially eased the pressure on exchange rate adjustment, but at the expense of a partial retrogression of market-oriented reform. The release of depreciation pressure helped reduce economic imbalances: the PPI reversed its decline and real interest rates fell sharply, easing deflationary pressure; capital outflows slowed significantly, and foreign reserves stabilized; stock market volatility fell and housing prices returned to a rising trend.

The three exchange rate adjustments effectively released, to varying degrees, the pressure from accumulated economic imbalances, mitigating the impact of the crises. The 1994 exchange rate reform effectively eased depreciation pressure on the exchange rate, corrected the current account deficit, reversed capital outflow pressure, and increased foreign reserves, significantly enhancing the economy's resilience against the 1997 Asian financial crisis. The 2005 exchange rate policy adjustment partially eased currency revaluation pressure, but the magnitude of the one-off revaluation was limited, and subsequent appreciation was slow and incomplete; hence, it was unable to alleviate the imbalances resulting from surging trade surplus and foreign capital inflows. It was not until the outbreak of the 2008 global financial crisis that appreciation pressure was temporarily reversed. Following the Federal Reserve's tapering announcement in 2013, international capital inflows began to recede. The USD entered an appreciation cycle, and pressure for RMB appreciation gradually switched to that of depreciation. A series of exchange rate policy adjustments that began in 2015 helped ease depreciation pressure, mitigate deflation and capital outflows, and reduce stock market volatility.

All three exchange rate policy adjustments showed that equilibrium exchange rates cannot be determined subjectively, and should be determined by the market. At the start of the 1994 exchange rate reform, many believed that it was difficult to maintain the unified rate of 8.7, and that the RMB would continue to depreciate. Much to the surprise of many, the RMB actually appreciated. Experiences from the 1994 exchange rate reform show that stabilizing the exchange rate as a means of instilling confidence is unnecessary: Under depreciation pressure, stabilizing the nominal exchange rate will not boost confidence but instead accelerate capital flight. Prior to the 2005 exchange rate reform, the RMB faced unilateral revaluation pressure, but even with a one-time appreciation of 2.1% as part of the reform, the RMB exchange rate still failed to reach equilibrium, embarking on a decade-long gradual appreciation path. Prior to the 2015 exchange rate reform, the USD/RMB exchange rate stabilized at the 6.1–6.2 level after years of appreciation. After the exchange rate reform, the USD/RMB central parity rate formation mechanism became increasingly market driven. The USD/RMB exchange rate, during its transition toward a new equilibrium, experienced depreciation-intervention-redepreciation over a three-year period, suggesting that the equilibrium exchange rate should not be based on subjective opinion or be artificially maintained by the government. Moreover, the equilibrium exchange rate does not remain unchanged: It adjusts constantly according to numerous factors, including changing economic and market environments both at home and abroad, and can only be determined by the dynamic interplay between market supply and demand.

FXIs during the three crises slowed macroeconomic self-adjustments, and the indirect economic costs incurred may have been underestimated or neglected. Although FXIs during the crises reduced nominal exchange rate volatility, it did not stop real exchange rates from adjusting through changes in domestic general and asset prices, which exacerbated the deflationary effect and increased systematic financial risks. The range of rescue measures and stimulus policies that followed suit increased the fiscal and debt burden of both the central and local governments, but the costs that stemmed in part from FXI were often underestimated or easily neglected.

Notes

1 Including a vast literature on the use of FXI for precautionary and mercantilist purposes (e.g., Aizenman and Lee, 2008; Jeanne and Ranciere, 2011; Ghosh et al., 2012).

2 Adler and Mano (2016) is a recent work that examines the quasi-fiscal costs associated with FXI.

3 Blanchard et al. (2015) focused primarily on the impact of FXI on exchange rates; we extend their methodology to examine other macroeconomic variables. In addition, we used "VIX" as our exogenous variable, which correlates highly with the capital flow measure constructed in Blanchard et al. (2015)and has been shown to yield similar empirical results.

4 As emphasized in Blanchard et al. (2015), the categorization is based on country responses to the specific choice of external shock only, or the "VIX" in our case. In practice, countries may also intervene in response to other types of shocks such as country-specific shocks.

5 Our sample is restricted, and like Blanchard et al. (2015),we exclude some country-specific periods of structural breaks related to changes in monetary and foreign exchange policies.

6 Inclusion of PPI is important in the computation of the real interest rate, as it more accurately captures the real lending/borrowing cost in the business loan market, which in many countries takes up a significant share of the overall credit market.

7 The number of lags for each individual VAR is based on the Akaike information criteria.

8 We choose not to include off-balance sheet items (derivatives) as they are not consistently available across countries and over time. Such items will be captured in the alternative FXI measure (Adler et al., 2021) that we use as a robustness check.

9 The weights are inversely proportional to the standard deviation of each impulse response.

10 A positive value implies depreciation.

11 Average year-over-year growth rate of CPI and PPI.

12   Canales-Kriljenko et al. (2003), Adler and Tova (2011), and Mohanty (2013) are examples of related work.

13   Their results show that for countries at the 75th percentile and 90th percentile, every 1%increase (as a share of GDP) in foreign reserve purchases (sales) will increase current account surplus (deficit) by 0.19% and 0.38% respectively.

14   One reason China's net external investment return has persistently remained in the negative region is that China's overall economic growth exceeds the average external growth; hence, average domestic investment returns are generally higher than external investment returns.

15   We use three-month moving averages of the data to smooth out the impulse response functions.

16   With the issuance of the *Public Announcement on Further Reforming the Foreign Exchange Management System* by the PBOC in 1994, a decision was made to implement a single managed floating exchange rate regime based on market supply and demand, and a two-tier structure comprising a market for FX settlement and sale via banks and an interbank FX market was created.

17   Since August 11, 2015, to reflect market supply and demand conditions, when lowering the central parity rate and guiding RMB depreciation, the authorities also stressed that reference should be made to the closing exchange rate of the previous day when determining future central parity rates. Elsewhere, to boost reference to the basket of currencies so as to better maintain the general stability of the RMB to the basket of currencies, CFETS released the CFETS RMB Index from December 11, 2015. The Index represented the value of the RMB versus a basket of currencies of 13 countries and regions, and served as a "currency basket". On this basis, the central parity rate formation mechanism made up of the "closing exchange rate + change in the exchange rates of the currency basket" was gradually established.

18   In May 2017, to duly offset the procyclical fluctuation of market sentiment, the PBOC changed the RMB/USD central parity rate quotation model from the original "closing exchange rate + change in the exchange rates of the currency basket" to "closing exchange rate + change in the exchange rates of the currency basket + counter-cyclical factor", with "counter-cyclical factor" being the adjustable component of the central parity rate formation mechanism. The "counter-cyclical coefficient" is set independently by quotation agencies based on changes in economic fundamentals and the procyclical extent of the FX market.

References

Adler, Gustavo, Chang, Kyun Suk, Mano, Rui, & Shaom, Yuting. 2021. Foreign exchange intervention: a dataset of public data and proxies. IMF Working Paper 21/047.

Adler, Gustavo, Lisack, Noemie, & Mano, Rui. 2015. Unveiling the effects of foreign exchange intervention: a panel approach. *Emerging Markets Review*, *40*, 100620.

Adler, Gustavo, & Mano, Rui. 2016. The cost of foreign exchange intervention: concepts and measurement. *Journal of Macroeconomics*, *67*, 103045.

Adler, Gustavo, & Tovar, Camilo E. 2011. Foreign exchange intervention: a shield against appreciation winds? IMF Working Paper 11/165.

Aizenman, Joshua, & Lee, Jaewoo. 2008. Financial versus monetary mercantilism: long-run view of large international reserves hoarding. *World Economy*, *31*(5), 593–611.

Alla, Zineddine, Espinoza, Raphael A., & Ghosh, Atish R. 2020. FX intervention in the New Keynesian Model. *Journal of Money, Credit and Banking, Blackwell Publishing*, *52*(7), 1755–1791, October.

Benes, Jaromir, Berg, A., Portillo, R., & Vavra, D. 2013. Modeling sterilized interventions and balance sheet effects of monetary policy in a new-Keynesian Model. IMF Working Paper 13/11.

Blanchard, Olivier J., Adler, Gustavo, & de Carvalho Filho, Irineu, Can foreign exchange intervention stem exchange rate pressures from Global Capital Flow Shocks? (July 2015). IMF Working Paper No. 15/159.

Blanchard, Olivier, Adler, Gustavo, & de Carvalho Filho, Irineu E. 2016. Can foreign exchange intervention stem exchange rate pressures from global capital flow shocks?" IMF Working Paper 15/159.

Branson, W.H., & Henderson, D.W. 1985. The specification and influence of asset markets. In R. W. Jones & P. B. Kenen (Eds.), *Handbook of international economics* (Vol. 2, ch. 15, pp. 749–805). Amsterdam: Elsevier.

Canales-Kriljenko, J.I. 2003. *Foreign Exchange Intervention in Developing and Transition Economies: results of a survey*. IMF Working Paper, 03/95, May.

Cavallino, Paolo. 2019. Capital flows and foreign exchange intervention. American Economic Journal: Macroeconomics, *11*(2), 127–170.

Chang, Roberto & Velasco, Andrés. 2017. Financial frictions and unconventional monetary policy in emerging economies. *IMF Economic Review, Palgrave Macmillan; International Monetary Fund*, *65*(1), 154–191, April.

Das, Mitali, Wang, Haobin, Li, Chuan, & Vargas, Mauricio. 2018. Returns of the external wealth of nations, Unpublished memo.

Das, Sonali. 2019. China's evolving exchange rate regime. IMF Working Paper 19/50.

Daude, Christian, Levy Yeyati, Eduardo, & Nagengast, Arne. 2014. On the effectiveness of exchange rate intervention in emerging markets. OECD Development Centre Working Paper 324.

Fanelli, Sebastián, & Straub, Ludwig. 2020. A theory of foreign exchange interventions. NBER Working Papers 27872, National Bureau of Economic Research.

Fratzscher, Marcel, Gloede, Oliver, Menkhoff, Lukas, Sarno, Lucio, & Stöhr, Tobias. 2019. When is foreign exchange intervention effective? Evidence from 33 countries. *American Economic Journal: Macroeconomics*, *11*(1), 132–156.

Gabaix, Xavier, & Maggiori, Matteo. 2015. International liquidity and exchange rate dynamics. *The Quarterly Journal of Economics*, *130*(3), 1369–1420.

Ghosh, Atish R., Ostry, Jonathan D., & Tsangarides, Charalambos G. 2012. Shifting motives: explaining the buildup in official reserves in emerging markets since the 1980s. IMF Working Paper 12/34.

Gourinchas, Pierre-Olivier, & Rey, Hélène. 2007. From world banker to world venture capitalist: U.S. external adjustment and the exorbitant privilege. In Richard H. Clarida (Ed.), NBER Books. *G7 current account imbalances: Sustainability and adjustment* (pp. 11–66). Cambridge, MA: National Bureau of Economic Research.

Henderson, Dale W., & Rogoff, Kenneth. 1981. New foreign asset positions and stability in a world portfolio balance model. International Finance Discussion Papers 178, Board of Governors of the Federal Reserve System (U.S.).

Hofman, David J., Chamon, Marcos, Deb, Pragyan, Harjes, Thomas, Rawat, Umang, &Yamamoto, Itaru. 2020. Intervention under inflation targeting – when could it make sense? IMF Working Paper No. 20/9.

Husain, Aasim M., Mody, Ashoka, & Rogoff, Kenneth S. 2005. Exchange rate regime durability and performance in developing versus advanced economies. *Journal of Monetary Economics, Elsevier*, *52*(1), 35–64, January.

International Monetary Fund (IMF). 2012. *Annual report on exchange arrangements and exchange restrictions.* Washington, DC: International Monetary Fund.

Jeanne, Olivier, & Ranciere, Romain. 2011. The optimal level of international reserves for emerging market countries: a new formula and some applications. *The Economic Journal*, *121*(555), 905–930.

Jin, Zhongxia, Zhao, Yue, & Wang, Haobin. 2021. *RMB: From marketization to internationalization.* Beijing: China Financial Publishing House (in Chinese).

Kouri, Pentti J.K. 1981. *Balance of Payments and the Foreign Exchange Market: A Dynamic Partial Equilibrium Model.* NBER Working Papers 0644, National Bureau of Economic Research, Inc.

Krznar, Ivo, & Kunovac, Davor. 2010. Impact of external shocks on domestic inflation and GDP. Working Paper 26, The Croatian National Bank, Croatia.

Mitali, Das, Li, Chuan, Vargas, Mauricio, & Haobin, Wang. 2020. Returns of the wealth of nations. Mimeo.

Mohanty, Madhusudan. 2013. Market volatility and foreign exchange intervention in EMEs: what has changed? BIS Papers No 73: 1–10, Basel: Bank for International Settlements.

Ostry, Jonathan D., & Ghosh, Atish R. 2009. Choosing an exchange rate regime. Finance and Development, *47*(4), 38–40.

Ostry, Jonathan D., Ghosh, Atish R., & Chamon, Marcos. 2015. Two targets, two instruments: monetary and exchange rate policies in emerging market economies. *Journal of International Money and Finance*, *60*, 172–196.

Phillips, Steven, Catão, Luis, Ricci, Luca, Bems, Rudolfs, Das, Mitali, Di Giovanni, Julian, Unsal, D. Filiz, Castillo, Marola, Lee, Jungjin, Rodriguez, Jair, & Vargas, Mauricio. 2013. The external balance assessment (EBA) methodology. IMF Working Paper 13/272.

Yi, Gang, & Tang, Xuan. 2001. A theoretical foundation of "corner solution assumption" of exchange rate regime. *Journal of Financial Research* (in Chinese), 8, 5–17.

2 Laying a Solid Foundation and Moving toward a Free-Floating Exchange Rate Regime

A Successful Floating Exchange Rate Regime Requires Good Monetary and Fiscal Discipline

Achieving Integration between Floating Exchange Rates and Currency Stability

Improving exchange rate flexibility has always been the direction of China's exchange rate reform. The 1994 exchange rate reform unified the RMB exchange rate. Upon unification, a single managed floating RMB exchange rate system based on market supply and demand was adopted (Guofa No. 89 [1993]). The 2005 reform of the RMB exchange rate formation mechanism launched China's managed floating exchange rate regime based on market supply and demand, and regulated with reference to a basket of currencies. The RMB exchange rate was no longer pegged solely to the USD, resulting in a more flexible RMB exchange rate mechanism (PBOC Announcement No. 16 [2005]). The 2015 exchange rate reform introduced a new central parity rate pricing mechanism that comprised "closing exchange rate + exchange rates of the currency basket", making the RMB more resilient and flexible. These steps show that continuously reforming the RMB exchange rate formation mechanism, making it evolve toward free-floating exchange rates, has always been a priority of the nation's market reform and opening up. This is particularly the case since 2016 as the monetary authority gradually withdrew from daily intervention in the FX market, and the exchange rate's resilience and flexibility increased significantly.

A more flexible exchange rate regime has more advantages than disadvantages. A more flexible exchange rate regime can adjust ongoing BOP imbalances on a real-time basis. This is a comprehensive adjustment targeted at the current account as well as the capital and financial accounts in the BOP, and adaptable to the new situation after the capital and financial accounts are liberalized, that is, the interaction between

DOI: 10.4324/9781003305668-2

the current account and the capital and financial accounts, as well as overall adjustments of the BOP as a whole. This can reduce, and even prevent, the macroeconomic cost brought about by FXI, as well as prevent macroeconomic risks that distort key domestic economic variables such as goods prices, real interest rates, and asset prices.

To be sure, the uncertainties caused by free-floating exchange rates may include risks, but most exchange rate volatility risks are common and can be managed by market mechanisms. Very few occasional excessive exchange rate volatility risks would cause economic and financial risks such as vicious depreciation of the home currency, hyperinflation, corporate bankruptcies, and capital outflows, but these outcomes are often not primarily the result of floating exchange rates, but of significant imbalances attributable to macroeconomic policies at home and abroad. When significant macroeconomic imbalances occur and cause considerable depreciation pressure on exchange rates, artificially maintaining exchange rate stability would be futile and would actually compound the loss. In countries where macroeconomic governance is more matured, exchange rate flexibility and stability can be unified. This offers not only market-driven flexibility but also comparative and dynamic stability on a flexible basis.

Of the existing international monetary systems, no universally accepted valuation benchmark such as gold exists. The level of goods prices and the economic cycle, among other factors, are also unlikely to be convergent across different countries. As an independent and enormous economy, it is also unlikely that China would join a currency zone dominated by another major currency. Against this objective backdrop, we must set aside the illusion of maintaining absolute bilateral nominal exchange rate stability, but adopt floating exchange rates. We should also ensure the stable purchasing power of our nation's currency against a basket of major goods by steadfastly adhering to prudent monetary and fiscal policies. This implies that the central bank must hold fast to its goals of price stability and financial stability.

Under the flexible exchange rate system, exchange rate stability is relative rather than absolute; it is not the result of intervention, and even more, not the unilateral decision of any country. As long as the currency of a country is not pegged to that of another, all that the country can do is to do its best to ensure stable real purchasing power of its currency. It cannot ensure the currency's stability against that of another country. Ultimately, the relative stability of a country's exchange rate depends on whether its monetary, fiscal, financial, and structural policies are robust; whether its current account and financial accounts are sound; and whether its debt levels and debt structure (type of currency and duration) are reasonable. These factors are critical to determining whether the macro-economy can withstand external shocks, and are also key to determining medium- and long-term exchange rates. Exchange rates will also be affected by investor sentiment, capital flows, financial market sentiment, and other factors.

To minimize risks to economic and financial stability as a result of exchange rate fluctuations, it is critical to establish comprehensive FX derivatives markets. The FX derivatives markets should have sufficient depth and breadth, and also cater to a wide range of market players. This will offer market players with FX risk exposure a comprehensive range of instruments, and will lower their cost of hedging against exchange rate volatility. Meanwhile, regulators should duly manage possible risks in the FX derivatives markets to prevent new risks arising from large volatility in the derivatives markets.

Meanwhile, the "reasonable and balanced" level of an exchange rate can change. The reasonable and balanced level of an exchange rate depends on the labor productivity as well as the monetary and fiscal conditions of the two countries concerned. It also depends on cross-border capital flows and other variables that will change over time and according to dynamic economic conditions, making real-time observation difficult. Hence, reasonable and balanced exchange rates cannot be accurately determined by humans in a subjective way; they can only be determined objectively via adjustments in the FX market. Exchange rates comprise both "nominal" and "real" definitions, and pegging one precludes pegging the other simultaneously. Pegging both at the same time is wishful thinking. Therefore, a reasonable and balanced level of exchange rate must ultimately be driven by market supply and demand.

One of the advantages of floating exchange rates is clear rules, which can be formulated by decision-making departments with expert assistance. Nonetheless, the level of daily exchange rates should be decided by the market. The government's role is to build and govern the market competently. Exchange rate is a highly specialized issue, but exchange rate policy decisions are normally made by politicians. Politicians can decide the mechanisms and rules for exchange rate formation based on scientific discussions, but making constant decisions on the specific level of exchange rates is not always possible.

Modern international financial knowledge should be popularized among different macroeconomic departments and major financial media. The public should be made aware that exchange rates should be market driven and that floating exchange rate risks should be managed by market-related means. In terms of publicity, the media and government documents should avoid providing misleading guidance that simply regards exchange rate appreciation or stability as success, and normal fluctuations or depreciation in the exchange rate as failures. Instead, they should educate the public to adopt a calm mindset by regarding normal exchange rate fluctuations as the norm, and unusually steady exchange rates as exceptions. Large bilateral nominal exchange rate volatility is not necessarily a bad thing. In media publicity, more attention should be paid to the domestic purchasing power of the home currency, and whether multilateral exchange rates and REER are relatively stable. Bilateral nominal exchange rate stability is not necessarily a good thing either. Exceptionally easy monetary policy adopted by foreign central banks can lead to a quietly sharp appreciation of the RMB's multilateral exchange rates or REER under a seemingly stable bilateral nominal exchange rate, thereby resulting in an unconscious buildup of depreciation pressure. REER data announced by the Bank for International Settlements (BIS) revealed that after the Federal Reserve's tapering in the second half of 2014, the RMB's REER appreciated sharply from 111.44 in July 2014 to 126.54 in July 2015, up by 13.5% in just one year. The seemingly stable nominal exchange rate masked the rapid buildup of depreciation pressure.

Different exchange rate regimes imply different sets of macropolicy rules. Choosing a stable RMB/USD bilateral exchange rate implies the need to accept upward or downward adjustments of domestic goods and asset prices in tandem with an increase or decrease in USD liquidity. Meanwhile, choosing floating exchange rates implies the automatic reaction of the exchange rate when USD liquidity increases or decreases. The impact on domestic goods prices must be dealt with by adjusting monetary policies in a targeted manner. Therefore, *prompt and adequate adjustments of domestic monetary policy should go hand in hand with floating exchange rates.*

Box 2.1 Successes and failures in moving toward free-floating exchange rates based on international experiences

In recent years, countries such as Argentina, Egypt, and Pakistan have faced economic challenges and applied for IMF programs. The IMF usually requires that borrowing countries meet certain policy conditions in many areas such as monetary, fiscal, financial, and structural reforms. In terms of exchange rates, the Fund usually requires the central bank of the borrowing country to reduce FXI and increase exchange rate flexibility. Based on outcome,

Egypt's program was very successful. Although the country's exchange rate depreciated by almost 50% initially, its central bank steadfastly refused to intervene. After the devaluation, the exchange rate remained stable and rebounded by nearly 10%, gradually helping Egypt move successfully toward a floating exchange rate regime (IMF, 2019a). *Pakistan*'s program is still ongoing (IMF, 2019d). Prior to and in the initial phase of the program, the Pakistani rupee (PKR) devalued by approximately 30% at one time, but inflation remained stable. As the program progressed, exchange rates bottomed and rebounded, and finally moved toward floating flexibly. In contrast, *Argentina*'s program is less than optimistic. The more than 40% devaluation of its currency during the program resulted in hyperinflation and highly elevated debt levels. The Argentinian government was forced to intervene in the FX market and to impose stringent capital controls (IMF, 2019b). Why do different countries witness differing outcomes as they move toward a floating exchange rate regime? What are the prerequisites for moving toward a floating exchange rate regime? Based on the experiences of the aforesaid countries, we believe that *the following three factors are critical to a successful exchange rate reform.*

1. Public debt levels, particularly external debt levels, must be well controlled. A comparison of the case studies between Egypt and Argentina shows that the two countries experienced significant devaluation at the start of their programs, but the economic impacts on the two countries were very different. After the Egyptian pound (EGP) devalued significantly by 50% between October and November 2016, it remained stable thereafter. The inflation rate rose to 30% at the end of 2016, and remained at that level for 10 months, before tight monetary policy gradually lowered the inflation rate to about 15%, which then remained generally stable. Egypt's external debt levels were relatively low compared to other emerging market economies. Public sector external debt was 7.8% of GDP in 2015. While this number rose to 18% in 2016 after the EGP devalued sharply, it was still within a well-controlled range. The exchange rate devaluation led to a dramatic improvement in the current account, with the current account deficit shrinking from 6% in 2015/16 to 2.6% in 2018/19. The effect of various economic reforms emerged over time, and the exchange rate began to appreciate gradually from the beginning of 2019. By end-2019, the EGP had appreciated by about 8%. During this process, the Egyptian central bank did not carry out any FXI, and the economy ran steadily. Thanks to the reforms, Egypt became the fastest-growing country in the region, with GDP growth at 5.6% in 2019. The country moved successfully toward a flexible floating exchange rate regime.

Meanwhile, Argentina's currency also devalued sharply at the start of its IMF program. From August to September 2018, the Argentine peso (ARS) devalued by 40%; the inflation rate stood at 47.6% in 2018, and remained thus. External debt comprised a very large proportion of Argentina's public debt. The devaluation of the ARS saw external debt leap from 40% of GDP in 2017 to 65.7% in 2018. The soaring debt burden significantly offset the advantages from the flexible exchange rate in improving the current account. With investors losing confidence in Argentina's debt service capacity, the ARS has, since July 2019, continued to devalue by 40%, while inflation rate rose further to 54%. The country endured large capital outflows during this process. To stabilize the economy, the Argentinian government was forced to carry out large-scale foreign exchange interventions and impose capital controls. The exchange rate reform failed.

The differing fortunes of Egypt and Argentina show that a well-controlled external debt level was a key determinant to the success of the IMF program. If a country's macro-economy is overly dependent on external debt, exchange rate devaluation could trigger an external debt service capacity crisis, thereby creating a vicious circle of currency devaluation – soaring external debt – capital flight. If a country's external debt levels are lower, currency devaluation may cause rising inflationary pressure in the short term, but tight monetary policy will play a role in ultimately lowering inflation rate and restoring market confidence. Improvement in the current account owing to currency devaluation will also help to drive economic growth.

2. Pre-reform exchange rate levels at close to or slightly below equilibrium (i.e., excessive depreciation or having overshot) facilitate steady implementation of reform. Compared to Egypt and Argentina, Pakistan's exchange rate reform was more prudent. Since the beginning of 2017, the PKR had already gradually devalued by 30%, and was basically at equilibrium prior to the start of the IMF program in July 2019. After the State Bank of Pakistan announced the adoption of floating exchange rates, the exchange rate quickly bottomed before rebounding. By the end of 2019, the PKR had already appreciated by about 6% from its trough in June 2019. Meanwhile, the inflation rate in 2018 stood at a controllable level of approximately 7.3%. Pakistan's public external debt was also relatively limited. During the currency devaluation phase, external debt of the public sector increased from 18.5% of GDP in 2017 to 24.4% in 2019, which was still under control. As the level of exchange rate prior to the reform was generally consistent with Pakistan's fundamentals, liberalizing the exchange rate did not result in a dramatic devaluation. According to the Pakistani authorities, successfully transforming into a market-determined exchange rate regime was key to the program's success. As the exchange rate moved toward a floating regime, the central bank of Pakistan tightened monetary policy, and kept real interest rate positive. At the same time, the central bank did not extend the maturity of maturing government bonds held, avoiding central bank financing. This further ensured tightened monetary policy. These measures effectively curbed inflation and successfully stabilized market sentiment, increasing foreign investors' confidence in investing in Pakistan's financial assets. The central bank's foreign reserves rose steadily.

3. The level of dollarization in the country cannot be excessive prior to successful exchange rate reform. Another reason why Argentina's exchange rate reform failed was because the economy was highly dollarized. The transactions of some key economic sectors (particularly fuel, electricity, and other energy payments) were priced in US dollars, as were government debt and foreign investments. The public's psychological pricing of goods and services were also in USD. This meant that exchange rate devaluation would directly lead to rising prices. The excessively high level of dollarization significantly weakened the effect of tightening monetary policy, and made the monetary policy tightening ineffective in curbing inflation. In fact, although the Argentinian authorities adopted a tight monetary policy, the sharp devaluation of the ARS caused fuel and electricity costs to increase from about 2% to 15% of corporate earnings, which quickly bankrupted many enterprises. Hence, for some Latin American countries that have relatively high levels of dollarization, "de-dollarization" may be a key condition for moving toward floating exchange rates.

Macro and Micro Conditions for Moving toward a Floating RMB Regime

In the course of moving toward a floating RMB regime, both macro- and microeconomic policy frameworks should be improved to ensure exchange rates float freely but not uncontrollably, and remain relatively stable while adjusting flexibly.

To achieve a relatively stable exchange rate under a more flexible exchange rate regime, major macroeconomic imbalances should be avoided and systemic risks in the financial system should be controlled. Macroeconomic and financial system vulnerabilities that have the biggest impact on exchange rates mostly come from three areas. *1.) External sector imbalances,* which include sustained large current account deficits, overreliance on short-term capital inflows, and foreign currency debt, among others. Experience suggests that external sector imbalances are often reflected in financial turbulence in emerging market economies. These could cause investors' confidence to collapse, capital inflows to reverse, and the exchange rate to severely devalue. *2.) Fiscal imbalance,* which will result in huge budget deficits and high public debt, crowding out private sector financing. Unsustainable government debt will ultimately result in inflation. If government debt also comprises massive external debt, severe fiscal imbalances will likely cause external default and exchange rate depreciation. *3.) Financial sector and corporate sector imbalances.* Excessive borrowing of large amounts of external debt is the biggest threat to exchange rate stability. During periods of external capital inflows or overheating in the economy, credit in the financial and corporate sectors would overexpand, and leverage and maturity mismatch would increase. Once the international financial environment tightens, capital outflow would occur and the currency would depreciate, decreasing corporate debt service capacity and increasing bank NPLs and capital inadequacy, triggering financial and currency crises.

International experience suggests that a healthy and stable macroeconomy is fundamental for achieving exchange rate flexibility without losing soundness. Hence, it is worth assessing China's overall economic soundness before the RMB exchange rate moves toward a flexible floating rate. In this regard, we adopt two sets of indicators to assess China's current macroeconomic health based on the IMF's method of assessing a country's economic soundness and systemic risk. The two indicators focus on different perspectives. They complement each other, and help to better reflect the full view of the soundness of China's macroeconomic conditions.

Macroeconomic Vulnerability Assessment Approach

This is a quantitative approach used to assess vulnerabilities. Based on a top-down approach, key macroeconomic indicators such as current account deficit to GDP, public debt to GDP, and NPL ratios of the financial sector have been selected from four sectors, namely, the external, public, financial, and corporate sectors. Some previous research shows that these key indicators will help to predict whether a country will have a financial crisis in two years' time (IMF, 2007, 2017). To assess China's overall economic condition, we compare China's various indicators against the safety thresholds set by the IMF and against the average levels of those indicators of emerging market economies around the world (Table 2.1).[1]

The impact of the external sector on exchange rates is more direct. The state of the current account as well as the capital and financial accounts will affect the relative demand for the currency of one country against that of other countries, thereby affecting exchange rates. *Next, the impact of the public, financial, and corporate sectors on exchange rates is primarily reflected through inflation expectations and the probability of external debt default.* A country's excessively high public debt, unsound financial system, or high NPL ratios could trigger investor concerns over inflation and lead to depreciation pressure on exchange rates. If a country's public and corporate sectors have high external debt levels that are unsustainable or at risk of default, capital inflows could stop abruptly and large capital outflows could occur, triggering a depreciation in exchange rates.

On the whole, China's external sector is relatively sound. In terms of foreign reserve adequacy, China's current foreign reserve adequacy, at approximately 2.5 times the safety threshold or about 1.7 times the average level of emerging markets, is relatively sound. However, given the deteriorating external environment now confronting China and increasing uncertainty, preparations for extreme situations should be made. As at end-2019, China's foreign reserves amounted to USD 3.1079 trillion, with foreign direct investment at USD 2.9281 trillion, and securities investment at USD 1.3646 trillion; current account surplus stood at USD 177.5 billion. Under extreme circumstances, even if one-third of direct investment and two-thirds of securities investment in China leave the country, and assuming that the current account is in a state similar to that in 2019, a rough calculation shows that China would have a BOP deficit of USD 1.5 trillion, accounting for approximately half of China's total foreign reserves. However, given that the actual available amount of foreign reserves in China is less than the

Table 2.1 A comparison of macroeconomic indicators and safety thresholds between China and other emerging markets

	Safety threshold	*2018 China data*	*2018 emerging market median data*	*Weight*
External sector				**0.45**
Foreign reserves as a percentage of the sum of external debt due within one year or less and current account deficit	>101	242	145	0.24
Current account surplus (% of GDP)	>–2.7	0.9	–2.7	0.25
External debt (% of GDP)	<32.8	13.3	60.8	0.05
External debt (% of exports)	<216	70	172	0.26
REER disequilibrium (% deviation from equilibrium)	Absolute value <6.4	0	na	0.2
Public sector				**0.25**
Fiscal surplus (% of GDP)	>–3.6	–2.7	na	0.2
Difference between fiscal surplus net of interest payments and sustainable level (% of GDP)	>–1.8	**–2.3**	–0.8	0.25
Public debt (% of GDP)	<25.6	**50.1**	56.9	0.15
Public debt with foreign exchange risk exposure (% of GDP)	<20.4	0.2	23.3	0.2
Public debt due within one year or less (% of GDP)	<10.5	7.2	8.4	0.2
Financial sector				**0.15**
Capital adequacy (%)	>12	14.2	16.5	0.22
Return on assets (ROA) (%)	>0.2	1.3	1.54	0.21
NPLs (% of total loans)	<4.9	1.8	na	0.2
Annual change in credit-to-GDP	<0.3	–0.4	na	0.12
Soundness of institutions – Dummy variable				0.25
Corporate sector				**0.15**
Interest coverage ratio	>6.5	43	32.1	

Source: IMF.

Note: The thresholds were last publicly disclosed by the IMF in 2007. To facilitate global comparison, the data the IMF collected this time was as at August 2018.

total amount of foreign reserves, relying on foreign reserves to stabilize the exchange rate may not be feasible under extreme circumstances.

From a BOP perspective, the current account remains in a surplus, better than the average levels of emerging market economies (current account deficit at 2.7% of GDP). External debt is just 13.3% of GDP, approximately one-third that of the safety threshold, and one-fifth of the average level of emerging markets. The external debt-to-export ratio is also far lower than the safety threshold and the average level of emerging markets. *In terms of the capital and financial accounts,* as China's financial sector gradually opens up, the magnitude of capital inflows and outflows under the capital account has grown. Taking into consideration that fluctuations in the capital and financial accounts are generally larger, strengthening macroprudential regulatory policies on the capital and financial accounts is critical. This is particularly the case when there are significant capital inflows, given that the BOP crisis of many countries originates from capital inflows. Although capital inflows would boost prices and economic prosperity initially, international capital fluctuations are cyclical, and future capital outflows are, by and large, inevitable.

In the context of the pandemic, if some countries were to adopt an extremely expansionary monetary policy that would benefit themselves at the expense of others, similar to that prior to World War II, this might cause depreciation of exchange rates of major currencies and massive low-cost capital inflows into China. China may also consider adopting measures to stem the deluge of capital inflow, but it does not need to purchase large amounts of foreign reserves through direct FXI; rather, this could be achieved by adopting macroprudential management measures, which would also conform to the IMF's "Institutional View" on capital flows.

Overall, China's external sector remains sound, even taking into consideration the current harsh export conditions, increasing capital market liberalization, and other factors. However, if exchange rates are to be rigidly defended, underlying vulnerabilities will be higher than those shown by the indicators. Flexible exchange rates can serve as shock absorbers, lowering the pressure of capital flows on the economy.

In terms of the public sector, China's total debt has risen rapidly but its debt service capacity remains sound. The pandemic has significantly increased China's latest fiscal deficit and government debt. The latest IMF figures reveal that China's augmented general government deficit (including estimated off-budget investment spending) was estimated to rise to 18.2% of GDP in 2020, up approximately 5.6 percentage points from that in 2019. The 2020 augmented general government debt (including estimated off-budget investment spending) to GDP ratio would rise to 92% from 76% in 2019, and will continue to rise over the medium term. We would like to highlight that the IMF's augmented general government debt figure could have exaggerated the size of China's government debt, because it included the debt of local government financing platforms not recognized by the central government as part of government debt, and it did not calculate net government debt. More importantly, although sharply higher leverage would, to a certain extent, increase public sector vulnerability, it may not necessarily cause a depreciation of the exchange rate. An exchange rate is the relative price between two currencies. Given that many major nations introduced fiscal stimuli during the pandemic, leverage ratios have increased for many. Therefore, one would not be able to conclude that the RMB would depreciate simply by looking at China's leverage ratios. Moreover, China's economy has recovered rapidly, and has become the first major economy in the world to achieve positive growth. This will help underpin the RMB. Meanwhile, external debt and short-term debt comprise a relatively low proportion of China's public debt. In addition, real economic growth is higher than real interest rates, and domestic savings, which account for about 43% of GDP, are being invested in the country. These all have a positive impact on public finance.

In terms of the proportion of foreign and short-term debt, public debt with foreign exchange exposure accounts for a mere 0.2% of GDP, far lower than the safety threshold of 20.4% and the 23.3% average of developing nations. Meanwhile, the short-term debt-to-GDP ratio is also lower than the safety threshold and that of other developing nations. *As for debt service capacity,* the key indicator for measuring debt sustainability is comparing the magnitude of real interest rate and real economic growth. If the real interest rate is lower than real GDP growth, even if the absolute value of a country's total debt to GDP ratio is higher, debt is still safe. China's 2019 public sector interest expense-to-GDP ratio was 1.04%, lower than the emerging market average of 2.7%, while real GDP growth was 6.6%, higher than the emerging market average of 3.2%. From this perspective, China's public debt sustainability remains relatively high. Elsewhere, income from assets in China's government balance sheet is relatively high, and net asset value is still positive. In 2017 (IMF's latest estimate), China's government net asset value-to-GDP ratio was 10.5%, and some of the debt pressure could be offset by asset returns.

The financial sector is generally sound with all indicators within the safety threshold, yet vulnerabilities do exist. China financial sector's risk weighted capital adequacy, at 14.2%, is higher than the safety level specified by the Basel Accords and the risk threshold calculated by the IMF, but lower than the average levels of developing countries. The financial sector's return on assets (ROA), at 1.3%, is higher than the 0.2% safety threshold, but slightly lower than the average levels of developing countries. The NPL ratio, at 1.8%, is within the safety threshold. The IMF's latest estimate shows that China's total bank NPLs rose by 18% year over year in H1 2020 because of the pandemic. A rising NPL ratio is a concern but a common phenomenon around the world at this stage. Hence, it is difficult to determine the trend of exchange rates solely based on this factor.

China's corporate sector has very little external debt. The country's main challenge is how to further boost SOE reforms. China's corporate sector external debt is just 1.4% of GDP, far lower than the international average. At present, the main challenges its corporate sector faces are continuing to deepen SOE reform and disposing of zombie enterprises. Research shows that the 20102017 ROA of China's SOEs was 7.5 percentage points lower than that of private enterprises over the same period. About one-third to a quarter of SOEs were loss-making, but these have not been shut down because of subsidies, regulatory forbearance, and government connections (IMF, 2020). Although the leverage ratios of Chinese enterprises have stabilized in the recent years, there is still room for improvement in terms of efficiency and corporate governance. The next step is to further implement the "competitive neutrality" principle, increase the effectiveness of SOE reform, improve market-oriented operating mechanisms, and increase core competitiveness.

Systemic Risk Tracker

The IMF recently established a new set of systemic risk trackers for individual countries. Using a bottom-up analysis framework, a set of key quantitative indicators covering the economic and financial sectors (such as the public sector, banking sector, non-bank financial institutions, and corporate sector), as well as financial markets (such as the bond market, stock market, foreign exchange market, and housing market) were selected to create a set of quantitative indicators to assess a country's systemic risk (IMF, 2019c). Compared to the aforesaid vulnerability assessment approach, the systemic risk trackers are based on data of specific economic and financial sectors, and are more focused on the segmental risk profile of and data trends in each sector. This enables regulators to take prompt action when risks first emerge, thus preventing individual risk from evolving into systemic risk.

On the basis of the aforesaid indicators, we make a quantitative comparison of the performance of each relevant sector between China and the G20 nations, by way of time series and cross-country comparisons as well as panel comparison. We then analyze the systemic risk confronting China and propose policy recommendations. The data comparison is set out in Table 2.2.

On the whole, none of the indicators shows that China has systemic risk, but some of the segmental risks should be monitored and promptly managed.

Public sector debt is under control, but external debt growth is gaining momentum and should be monitored. Government debt-to-GDP ratio, at 50.6%, is higher than the 36% of G20 nations, but remains relatively lower on an international basis. Nonetheless, compared to China's own data, this figure has exceeded 93% of the country's historical period, and is at a historic high. External debt as a proportion of government debt is relatively small, lower than 94% of G20 nations. It is worth pointing out that RMB external debt comprises a portion of China's total external debt. Compared to foreign currency external debt, the risk of the RMB external debt is more controllable. However, China's external debt growth is gaining momentum, and the growth rate is ahead of G20 nations. This is all the more prominent given that the US and European nations are at zero or even negative interest rates. Hence, preventing and controlling the risk of excessive external debt growth is a necessary precaution so as to ease large-scale debt service pressure in the event of rising interest rates in the future.

There is as yet no financial sector systemic risk, but default probability among financial institutions is high and should be monitored. China's 2018 credit-to-GDP ratio is 4.3 percentage points higher than its long-term trend, and higher than 63% of G20 nations. Compared to its own historical trend, however, this ratio has slowed, just 36% higher than its historical period. The risk-weighted capital adequacy ratio of deposit-taking institutions in China is higher than the safety level specified by the Basel Accords, and remains low compared to international levels, just higher than 23% of G20 nations. The ROA of deposit-taking institutions, at 0.9%, is slightly lower than the international average, underperforming 60% of G20 nations. However, China's NPL, loan provisions, and liquidity conditions are better than the international average. It is worth noting that the probability of default for China's financial institutions based on the bottom-up default analysis (BuDA) model is far higher than international peers, with default probability of non-bank financial institutions better than just 2% of countries. In this regard, credit risk should be closely monitored.

Table 2.2 China's systemic risk tracker: time series and cross-country comparisons

China's systemic risk tracker: Development trends and international comparison

	China Q4 2018 figure	International comparison: Comparison of G20 nations in 2018 (100 represents highest risk)	Comparison over time: Comparison of China's 2000–2018 data (100 represents highest risk)	Panel Comparison: Comparison of 2000–2018 data of G20 nations (100 represents highest risk)
Public sector				
General government gross debt-to-GDP ratio (%)	50.6	36	93	44
Government sector external debt to total government sector debt (%)	3.6	6	95	2
Annualized growth of real external debt of government sector (%)	41.8	96	77	96
Financial sector				
Difference between credit-to-GDP ratio and its long-term trend value (%)	4.3	63	36	58
Capital to risk-weighted assets of deposit-taking institutions (%)	14.2	77	2	68
Net foreign exchange exposure to capital of deposit-taking institutions (%)	-2.4	57	8	50
ROA of deposit-taking institutions (%)	0.9	59	94	61
Current assets to short-term liabilities of deposit-taking institutions (%)	55.3	39	7	42
Non-performing assets ratio (%)	1.8	44	95	32

(*continued*)

Table 2.2 Cont.

China's systemic risk tracker: Development trends and international comparison

	China Q4 2018 figure	International comparison: Comparison of G20 nations in 2018 (100 represents highest risk)	Comparison over time: Comparison of China's 2000–2018 data (100 represents highest risk)	Panel Comparison: Comparison of 2000–2018 data of G20 nations (100 represents highest risk)
3-year ahead cumulative probability of default of non-bank institutions based on the BuDA model (basis points)	194.3	98	19	89
Corporate sector				
Corporate sector external debt to GDP ratio (%)	1.4	4	53	0
3-year ahead cumulative probability of default of listed companies based on the BuDA model (basis points)	112.3	75	27	60
Short-term external debt as a percentage of corporate sector external debt (%)	34.5	83	53	73
Real growth rate of corporate sector external debt (%)	26.5	91	74	92
Financial market				
10-year government bond yield less CPI year-on-year growth rate (%)	3.5	44	61	69
Volatility of stock market returns	24.7	90	67	74
REER appreciation (annualized) (%)	-1.7	38	28	37
Volatility against the USD exchange rate	4.6	23	98	27

Housing market

Real house price growth (annualized) (%)	-4.4	7	6	11
House price-to-rent ratio (2008=100)	135	77	85	93
House price-to-income ratio (2008=100)	63.6	5	8	3

Source: IMF.

Note: The international comparison compares the 2018 data between China and G20 nations. The values of the same indicator for each country are ranked from the lowest to the highest in terms of risk, and the quantiles, identified (for instance, a quantile of 20 means that the risk of 20% of the countries in the sample has lower risks than the particular country). Time series comparison compares the quarterly data of China from 2000 to 2018. The values of the same indicator for different quarters are ranked from the lowest to the highest in terms of risk, and the quantiles, identified. The panel comparison compares the 2000–2018 data of all G20 nations. The values of the same indicator for each country and each quarter are ranked from the lowest to the highest in terms of risk, and the quantiles, identified.

The real sector and financial markets face less risk than the financial sector. The corporate sector's external debt-to-GDP ratio, at 1.4%, is far lower than that of most G20 nations, but real growth has been rapid in recent years, which deserves more attention. *In terms of financial markets,* real returns in the bond market are basically similar to those of the international average. Real stock market returns are far lower than the international average,[2] and volatility is higher. Foreign exchange market volatility has risen in recent years but is still lower than the international average.

In terms of the housing market, recent real house price growth has been lower than the international average. The 2018 national real house price index growth, at -4.4%, was just higher than a few G20 nations. Against international levels, China's house price-to-rent ratio has grown rapidly in recent years, faster than most G20 nations, but the growth rate of the house price-to-income ratio is higher than just a handful of G20 nations. On a nationwide basis, the 2018 house price-to-income ratio is just 63.6% of that in 2008.

It is worth noting that the moderate systemic risk in China's economy at this time indicated by the aforesaid assessment has been evaluated on the basis that the capital account has not been fully liberalized. In the process of gradually liberalizing the capital account and pushing ahead structural reform, exchange rates will adjust accordingly. A certain gap may exist between the final level of the exchange rate and the current level, but the magnitude of the gap is still uncertain at this time. Current policies limiting capital outflows have, to a certain extent, limited capital outflows. Therefore, capital controls should be liberalized gradually so that the impact of exchange rates on capital flows can be adapted and adjusted gradually. In the process of gradually liberalizing capital controls, two-way capital flows will become the norm. Volatility in the balance sheet of various economic sectors and market sentiment will increase. Therefore, further increasing the soundness of China's financial system is crucial to achieving full flexible floating exchange rates.

Meanwhile, when assessing the impact of a country's systemic risk on exchange rates, foreign currency risk and domestic currency risk should be differentiated. A portion of domestic currency risk can be resolved by the central bank by way of monetization. However, as this portion of the risk may ultimately trigger depreciation in the exchange rate, it should be avoided under normal circumstances. Even if it has to be ultimately used, such monetization would best be carried out when the economy is under deflationary pressure. Another part of the domestic currency risk can be resolved by way of domestic resource reallocation with little impact on a country's exchange rates.

A successful move toward free-floating exchange rates requires monetary policy "resoluteness". As mentioned previously, free-floating exchange rates referred to herein do not equate to a hands-off approach; rather, the floating exchange rates are based on rigorous macroeconomic policy discipline. Many emerging market economies experience significant currency depreciation, and even currency crises, in the process of moving toward a floating exchange rate regime. A key reason is the continued buildup of imbalances, which causes an inevitable collapse of the exchange rate when it approaches a certain level. This is not the ideal path of moving to a free-floating regime. To ensure both flexibility and stability in the exchange rate, the policy maker must diligently prevent significant imbalances from building up. This is very demanding of the policy makers in the performance of their duties.

Based on international experience, three items play a key role in the macroeconomic risk management of policy makers under a floating exchange rate regime: ability to keep money supply under control; ability to keep government debt, particularly net debt, under control; and ability to control total external debt, including the size of short-term external debt. The significance of the other items is determined based on the extent to which they relate to the aforesaid three items. Out of the three key items, the ability to control money supply is the most crucial, and reflects the "resoluteness" of monetary policy. It is also the most important representation of monetary policy independence. This demands that the institution responsible for the monetary policy of a country be free from interference from other departments. International experience has shown that developed countries normally ensure resoluteness and independence of monetary policy by legal and institutional means.

Compared to many countries around the world, China's current macro-economy is generally sound with relatively low economic vulnerabilities. Its external sector, in particular, is fairly robust. Over the medium to long term, whether financial sector and corporate sector risks will become BOP risks and affect the exchange rate is still dependent on the effectiveness of deepening structural reform. Meanwhile, an exchange rate is the pricing comparison between two currencies. It is not only determined by China's economic growth, but also that of the US, Europe, Japan, and other major economies. China's economy may have various problems, but this does not imply that the RMB will depreciate in the medium to long term because the economies of its major counterparties also have their own problems. The economic strength of China and other countries may change and switch. It is precisely because of these uncertainties that any attempt to stabilize the exchange rate at a particular rate by means of human intervention is impractical. The exchange rate will only be able to find its place through continuous overshooting and trial and error by the market. Any sustained large-scale intervention will do more harm than good.

It is worth highlighting that the discussion in this chapter about the macro and micro conditions for free-floating exchange rates is in the hope that after a floating exchange rate regime is adopted, large and dramatic volatility can be avoided However, this does not mean that floating rates cannot be achieved if the aforesaid macro and micro conditions are not met. In fact, even if a country's economic fundamentals are deteriorating and favorable macro and micro conditions no longer exist, flexible exchange rates remain important. This is because deteriorating economic fundamentals will result in significant BOP imbalances in a country, and flexible exchange rates can help rapidly restore the balance. Moreover, rigid exchange rates will only exacerbate BOP imbalance. Even if a sharp depreciation occurs after exchange rates are liberalized, this is the result rather than the cause of deteriorating economic fundamentals. Under these circumstances, a depreciation of the exchange rate will help the economy recover more quickly so that long-term economic growth can be achieved.

Mitigating Balance Sheet Effects When Implementing a Floating Exchange Rate Regime

According to conventional theories, the depreciation of exchange rates affects economic growth through the income effect and the substitution effect. The income effect of exchange rate depreciation functions as follows: When the exchange rate depreciation leads to an increase in total income, this in turn raises total demand, which has an expansionary effect on economic growth. For instance, sustained depreciation of the real exchange rate of developing countries can help increase trade sector income, which in turn promotes economic growth, rendering exchange rate depreciation an expansionary effect (Rodrik, 2008). Meanwhile, in scenarios where exchange rate depreciation does not increase total demand, it can have a contractionary effect on economic growth. Large currency devaluations, and even currency crises, will lead to changes in income distribution. The Mexican peso crisis, for instance, led to enormous income distribution imbalance at the micro level (Cravino and Levchenko, 2017) by transferring real purchasing power to those with higher marginal propensity to save. This led to higher savings and lower total demand, and caused real output and imports to decline after the event (Krugman and Taylor, 1978).

The substitution effect of an exchange rate is known as the expenditure switching effect in international macroeconomics (Engel, 2002). If domestically produced goods and imported goods are not perfect substitutes, then terms of trade will improve with currency appreciation. That is, the higher price of exports relative to the price of imports causes domestic demand to switch toward imports; in contrast, currency depreciation causes demand to switch toward domestic goods. Therefore, currency depreciation helps stimulate a country's tradable sector. Meanwhile, rising tradable sector demand increases wage levels and causes labor to flow from non-tradable sectors to tradable sectors, lifting tradable sector employment.

In sum, conventional theories argue that exchange rate depreciation helps promote tradable sector growth, which will in turn drive the economy (hereinafter referred to as the exchange rate "stimulus" channel). As such, when a country is confronted with external shocks resulting in a deterioration of BOP, exchange rate depreciation often plays the role of a "stabilizer", becoming the first line of defense against shocks.

Several recent studies have shown that dominant currency pricing could weaken the stimulus effect of exchange rate depreciation on the economy. It is suggested that under the current international currency system with USD being the dominant currency for bilateral trade, a depreciation in the domestic currency does not affect USD-denominated export prices, thereby weakening the stimulus effect of exchange rate depreciation on exports (IMF, 2019). Under the dominant currency pricing model, the magnitude of world trade is more affected by the value of the USD. A depreciation of the USD will boost the imports and exports of the US and other countries simultaneously, expanding world trade, while an appreciation of the USD will reduce the imports and exports of the US and other countries simultaneously, causing world trade to contract (Gopinath et al., 2020). However, the results of these studies merely show that a time lag exists between the timing of an exchange rate change and its effect on BOP. They do not deny the effect of flexible exchange rates in adjusting BOP. We can even be persuaded to believe that because a time lag exists, the more timely the exchange rate adjusts, the better.

Other studies have shown that under certain conditions, the traditional exchange rate depreciation stimulus channel not only has limited impact in the short term, but exchange rate depreciation may also have a negative impact on the economy through the balance sheet effect (Culiuc, 2020). The balance sheet channel effect states that when a country's foreign currency debt is high, the debt burden of domestic borrowers will increase because of the currency depreciation, thereby shrinking the net value of their balance sheet. The decrease in the net value of the balance sheet is further magnified by the financial system, thus constraining their ability to borrow (Gertler and Bernanke, 1989). Meanwhile, domestic banks with foreign currency debt will also have less ability to lend. In addition, foreign investors that hold the local currency bonds of that country will also see their assets contract in value, and reduce their holdings of that country's assets. The domestic losses because of the reduction in asset value, borrowing capacity, and bank lending capability, as well as reduction of domestic assets by foreign investors in the aforesaid channel may be regarded as the negative impact of exchange rate depreciation on a country's economy through the balance sheet channel (Mendoza and Smith, 2006; Mendoza, 2010).

The balance sheet effect produced by an exchange rate change is often immediate, but its stimulative effect on imports and exports is often reflected over time (Culiuc, 2020). There are four reasons for this: First, as major exports are denominated in USD, a depreciation in the domestic currency will not be directly passed through to changes in export prices. Rather, this will be reflected in the income of exporters, but there is a time lag before the exporters' income passes through to economic stimulation. Second, enterprises know that exchange rates will overshoot before gradually returning to equilibrium, and the equilibrium is what determines the investment returns of enterprises over the longer term. Therefore, enterprises will adopt a wait-and-see approach before making an investment decision. Third, the balance sheet effect indicates that even if exporters are willing to increase investment, banks are less willing to lend because of the damage to their balance sheet, thus affecting the availability of funds to exporters. Fourth, labor and other resources will not be able to shift immediately to the export sector due to stickiness in the economy, thereby causing a certain lag in the impact of exchange rate depreciation on imports and exports.

For countries with high foreign currency debt, the negative impact of exchange rate depreciation through the balance sheet channel often dominates the positive stimulus channel in the short term. While the stimulative effect is reflected only over time, the balance sheet effect is often immediate. Therefore, under existing accounting rules, when overshooting occurs, the negative impact of exchange rates on the economy through the balance sheet channel is often determined by the lowest exchange rate, that is, the exchange rate at the time overshooting occurred. In traditional channels, however, the stimulative effect of exchange rates on the economy is likely determined by the exchange rate when it returns to the equilibrium. Therefore, in the short term, the negative impact of exchange rates on the economy through the balance sheet channel can dominate the positive simulative effect.

In the medium term, however, exchange rate depreciation still has an overall positive impact on the economy. Empirical research shows that the degree of overshooting is primarily affected by a country's foreign reserves, trade openness, and size of external debt. The higher the reserves and the more open trade is, the lower the degree of overshooting. Meanwhile, the bigger the size of external debt, the higher the degree of overshooting. This result is relatively intuitive. A country's foreign reserves, trade openness, and size of external debt will affect investor confidence in the economy, thereby having an impact on the initial magnitude of depreciation of the exchange rate. Empirical research also indicates that in the short term, exchange rate depreciation has a negative impact on the economy, mainly because the balance sheet channel dominates. In the medium term, however, exchange rate depreciation has a positive impact on the economy. By then, the stimulative effect of the exchange rate on the economy often dominates.

In sum, to fully leverage the role of the flexible exchange rate regime as a "stabilizer", exchange rates should first be adjusted promptly to buy time for the lag in exchange rate pass-through; and second, excessive external debt and significant currency mismatch should be avoided. If a country has excessive external debt and significant currency mismatch, then the impact of exchange rate volatility, particularly the exchange rate depreciation, on the economy may be more negative than positive. On the other hand, if a country has well-controlled external debt and limited currency mismatch, then even a significant correction in the exchange rate would not be disconcerting. This conclusion further highlights the significance of macroprudential policies. The negative impact of exchange rate depreciation is often magnified through underlying financial sector risks. If exchange rate collapses along with a crisis in the banking system, the ultimate impact on the economy would be significant. Therefore, as China moves toward floating exchange rates, it should also adopt comprehensive macro and micro policy measures to strengthen the stability of the financial system, avoid excessive foreign currency debt, and prevent the formation of large-scale balance sheet effect.

Overcoming the "Fear of Floating": Individual Countries' Experience

Emerging market countries have always been conservative about implementing a floating exchange rate regime. This is also referred to as the "fear of floating" (Reinhart and Calvo, 2002), and is attributable to the following reasons: First, exchange rate volatility may bring about risk to enterprises with larger external debt exposure, particularly those with significant currency mismatch. Second, exchange rate volatility will increase the real cost of trading enterprises. Third, some worry that large exchange rate volatility will affect the implementation of monetary policy. For instance, it does not facilitate the implementation of inflation targeting.

Having implemented a floating exchange rate regime over the two decades, Chile has resolved the aforesaid "fear of floating" and has effectively increased its economy's ability to navigate external shocks. This is mainly reflected in the following areas:

First, the implementation of the floating exchange rate regime helped domestic enterprises actively reduce the proportion of USD debt. The proportion of enterprises using FX derivatives has also risen, reaching an estimated 60% in 2017 (Albagli et al., 2020). The FX derivatives market has grown rapidly and is nearly 10 times the size of 20 years ago, effectively mitigating risks caused by external debt exposure and currency mismatch.

Second, the implementation of floating exchange rates reduced monetary policy constraints, allowing the Central Bank of Chile to effectively implement inflation targeting and stabilize inflation expectations. Albagli et al. (2020) showed that following the adoption of a floating exchange rate regime, imported inflation into Chile has continued to weaken, and the sensitivity of import prices and domestic goods prices to exchange rate volatility has continued to decline, indicating that the central bank's credibility is rising.

Third, exchange rate flexibility has effectively increased Chile's ability to adjust to macro shocks. By comparing Chile's recovery following the 1997 Asian financial crisis and the 2008 Global financial crisis, Albagli et al. (2020) found that the implementation of floating exchange rates has helped Chile recover faster since the second financial crisis. Meanwhile, cross-country comparison also revealed that Chile's post-crisis recovery performance was better than other emerging market countries. Empirical results also showed that exchange rate adjustments had absorbed most of the impact of the Federal Reserve's monetary policy and global market uncertainty on Chile's asset prices, acting as a "stabilizer".

Overcoming the "Fear of Exchange Rate Overshooting"

For countries that have not adopted a floating exchange rate regime, one of the opposing views comes from the fear of "exchange rate overshooting". This view believes that an equilibrium exchange rate level exists, and if the current exchange rate is higher (or lower) than the equilibrium, the local currency is overvalued (or undervalued). According to this viewpoint, once allowed to float freely, exchange rates will depreciate (appreciate) significantly, and the magnitude will exceed the equilibrium exchange rate level, resulting in "exchange rate overshooting", and this "overshooting" is irrational. Therefore, a central bank will have to prevent exchange rate overshooting through FXI, or make a direct one-time adjustment, manually fixing the exchange rate at the equilibrium level. However, in practice, market intervention based on this viewpoint often fails.

In fact, exchange rate overshooting is the path that must be taken so that an equilibrium exchange rate may be revealed. The market, in the course of moving from the old to the new equilibrium, requires a continuous process of trial and error. Exchange rate equilibrium will only be ultimately determined through repeated price fluctuations. The exchange rate fluctuations are a necessary process for the price to explore and search for the equilibrium. The fluctuation is also convergent rather than divergent. In addition, the equilibrium exchange rate is not determined by one or two market players, nor manually set by a policy maker. It is determined by the entire market through continuous price adjustments. The "fear of exchange rate overshooting" view is in essence the hope of substituting market judgment for subjective judgment, replacing market-driven rates with government intervention.

On a theoretical basis, overshooting is determined by market forces. There are two prevailing theories on exchange rate overshooting. The first was first proposed by Dornbusch in 1976. This theory proposes that if there is an unanticipated permanent increase in the money supply, assuming sticky prices exist in the economy and output cannot be adjusted promptly in the short term, then interest rates will fall, thereby boosting demand for money. Based on the theory of interest rate parity, if a country's interest rate falls relative to that of other countries, investors must have currency appreciation expectations; otherwise, arbitrage opportunities will occur. Meanwhile, a permanent rise in money supply will cause that country's currency to depreciate (assuming long-term currency neutrality). Therefore, the only possibility is that the magnitude of the exchange rate depreciation must be large enough to generate appreciation expectations, thus resulting in "exchange rate overshooting". At a deeper level, this theory suggests that the essence of exchange rate overshooting is that if slow variables do not adjust (such as prices and output not being able to adjust in the short term), then fast variables (exchange rate) must overadjust (i.e., overshoot) so that overall equilibrium in the economy may be achieved.

The second exchange rate overshooting theory views the exchange rate as an asset price. According to the asset price bubble theory, if rational investors think that other investors believe asset prices will rise, they will buy assets and continue to drive asset prices higher even though current asset prices have already deviated from equilibrium. This herd effect and speculation may promote the formation of asset bubbles, causing the price to deviate from equilibrium.

Regardless of which overshooting theory we use, we find that exchange rate overshooting is a universal pattern of market price discovery, and current overshooting theories cannot provide an exhaustive explanation for the various overshooting phenomena in the market. Only through overshooting can market investors know the magnitude of the market's tension. The larger the exchange rate overshooting, the larger the bounce back to exchange rate equilibrium. From this perspective, the process of floating exchange rate fluctuations is a course of continuous overshooting and price discovery. Some theoretical studies have demonstrated that exchange rate intervention by central banks cannot eliminate exchange rate overshooting behavior (Sergio, 2007). Even if a central bank were to make a one-time administrative exchange rate adjustment to what it deems to be the "long-term equilibrium" level, that level will very possibly not be acknowledged by the market. The equilibrium exchange rate is the dynamically evolving continuous function. Therefore, the probability of manually adjusting the exchange rate to the appropriate equilibrium level is almost nil.

Box 2.2 Why a currency board regime is applicable to Hong Kong but not to mainland China

In Hong Kong SAR, the USD-based currency board regime, with the Hong Kong dollar pegged to the USD at a fixed rate, has performed well over the past decades. It has withstood many tests including the stock market crash of 1987, the 1994–1995 Mexican peso crisis, the 1997 Asian financial crisis, and the 2008 global financial crisis. Some argue that the currency board regime stabilizes confidence and reduces uncertainty in Hong Kong's economic activities. Hence, mainland China should learn from Hong Kong and maintain a stable exchange rate against the USD. This view, however, neglects major differences between Hong Kong and mainland China in many areas such as price flexibility, currency issuance base, and connection with the US economic and financial systems. These differences have determined that a currency board regime is perhaps applicable to Hong Kong but not mainland China.

First, without exchange rates functioning as the "automatic stabilizer", prices of goods, labor, and capital in the economy can only adjust automatically with capital flow cycles. Between 2012 and 2015, Hong Kong's economic growth lingered at a low of around 2% to 3%, and recovery prospects were uncertain. The US economy, on the other hand, had continued to recover from 2013, with Q3 2015 year-on-year GDP growth returning to the pre-crisis level of 2.1%. Under the currency board regime, however, the HKD appreciated passively in 2015 along with the USD, hurting its trade competitiveness. This triggered large corrections in Hong Kong's commodity, property, and equities prices not seen since 2016, as well as civil servant salary cuts and unemployment rise. As a small economy, Hong Kong has stronger tolerance for rapid downward price adjustments in the short term. For large economies, however, large downward fluctuations of domestic goods and asset prices may cause social upheaval. Therefore, leveraging the effect of flexible exchange rates as the automatic economic stabilizer is critical for large economies.

Second, mainland China and the US have different economic cycles. China must have its own independent monetary policy, and cannot choose to completely integrate into the US economy. Hong Kong, as an international financial center, may choose to be highly integrated with the US financial market at a particular time in history. Hong Kong's currency board regime is in essence a system with the USD as underlying currency. When HKD currency is issued, an amount of USD equivalent to the exchange rate of HKD 7.80 to USD 1 must be deposited with the Hong Kong Monetary Authority to support the issuance of HKD. This mechanism determines the basis for Hong Kong's currency board regime. The RMB, however, is an independent currency, and cannot make the USD the basis of issuance. Money supply in mainland China is determined by actual domestic conditions rather than the size of USD foreign reserves. Therefore, Hong Kong's foreign reserves are very large relative to the size of broad money, creating the necessary support for a fixed exchange rate system. Ultimately, the stability of the RMB exchange rate is not dependent on the size of foreign reserves but on the stability of the relationship between total

RMB issued and the corresponding total amount of goods and services.

In addition, the US accounts for a different proportion of economic activity in mainland China and in Hong Kong. It is very unlikely that China will choose a development path that integrates into the US economy. For the first five months of 2020, the US, having fallen in its rankings, became China's third-largest trading partner after the Association of Southeast Asian Nations (ASEAN) and the European Union (EU), with total China–US trade at RMB 1.29 trillion, accounting for 11.1% of China's total foreign trade value. In terms of direct investment, relevant reports cited on the official website of China's Ministry of Commerce reveal that direct investment in the US by Chinese enterprises fell to USD 5 billion (equivalent to approximately RMB 35.7 billion) in 2019, a new low in a decade. Therefore, whether the RMB exchange rate is stable or not cannot be assessed solely on bilateral exchange rates with the USD but on multilateral exchange rates based on a basket of currencies.

It is forecast that the US will likely feature less in China's external trade and investment going forward. The link between the US economy and China's economy is forecast to decline further, and a link between the RMB and the USD also lacks an economic basis. Hong Kong, meanwhile, is dominated by the financial services sector, and its financial links with Europe and the US are very much closer. One of the purposes of the HKD-USD peg is to maintain international investor confidence as regards the link between Hong Kong and the financial systems of Europe and the US.

Gradual appreciation (depreciation) cannot prevent overshooting. Instead, it may trigger greater overshooting because the exchange rate will be in a state of depreciation or appreciation for a longer period without reaching equilibrium. Hence, massive covered interest arbitrage occurs at each point in time and each price prior to the exchange rate reaching equilibrium, boosting depreciation or appreciation momentum. In other words, compared to a rapid depreciation (appreciation) of the exchange rate all the way to equilibrium, a gradual depreciation (appreciation) causes trading volume to increase sharply at each price point prior to reaching equilibrium.

The more flexibly exchange rates can be adjusted on a daily basis, the more likely it can avoid a significant one-time correction. If a central bank often maintains exchange rate stability through intervention, it may cause a continuous buildup of the nominal exchange rate and REER deviation. Once the exchange rate needs to be liberalized, a significant correction may very well be unavoidable. Therefore, to avoid large exchange rate volatility, the norm should be to allow the exchange rate to float on a daily basis, rather than make significant one-time exchange rate adjustments. Even in times of crisis, exchange rate intervention should not last too long. Otherwise, imbalances may continue to accumulate and expand due to the loss of valuable market information.

Notes

1 The safety threshold is calculated by minimizing the probability of prediction error, i.e., the sum of minimized probability of missing a crisis (number of times the value was higher than the safety threshold but a financial crisis occurred divided by total number of times a crisis occurred) and probability of a false alert (number of times the value was lower than the safety threshold but a financial crisis did not occur divided by total number of times a crisis did not occur). As the probability of the occurrence of a crisis is relatively low, this approach ensured that the damage from a missed crisis is far larger than the damage caused by a false alert.
2 In the systemic risk metrics, real stock market returns is measured based on the stock market index divided by the annualized growth rate of CPI. The lower the real stock market returns, the lower the mispricing risk.

References

Adrian, Tobias & Shin, Hyun Song. 2014. Procyclical leverage and value-at-risk. *Review of Financial Studies, 27,* 373–403.

Ahuja, Ashvin, Syed, Murtaza, & Wiseman, Kevin. 2017. Assessing country risk – selected approaches – reference note. IMF Technical Notes and Manuals 2017/008.

Albagli, Elias, Calani, Mauricio, MetodijHadzi-Vaskov, Metodij, Marcel, Mario, & Luca Antonio Ricci, Luca. 2020.Comfort in floating: taking stock of twenty years of freely-floating exchange rate in Chile. CEPR Discussion Paper, No. 14967.

Bems, Rudolfs, & di Giovanni, Julian. 2016. Income-induced expenditure switching. *American Economic Review, 106*(12), 3898–3931.

Bernanke, Ben S. & Gertler, Mark. 1989. Agency costs, net worth and business fluctuations. American Economic Review, *79*(1), 14–31.

Blanchard, Olivier, Adler, Gustavo, & de Carvalho Filho, Irineu E. 2015. Can foreign exchange intervention stem exchange rate pressures from global capital flow shocks? IMF Working Paper, No. 15/159.

Carlson, John A. & Osler, Carol L. 2000. Rational speculators and exchange rate volatility. *European Economic Review, 44*(2), 231–253.

Cravino, Javier & Levchenko, Andrei A. 2017. The distributional consequences of large devaluations. *American Economic Review*, November, 107(11), 3477–3509.

Culiuc, Alexander. 2020. Real exchange rate overshooting in large depreciation: determinants and consequences. IMF Working Paper No. 20/60.

Da Silva, Servio. 2001. Overshooting and foreign exchange intervention in the Redux model. Working Paper. http://www.angelfire.com/id/SergioDaSilva/ofredux.pdf

Doblas-Madrid, Antonio. 2011. A theory of speculative bubbles and overshooting during currency crises. Working Paper. Microsoft Word - Bubbles_CC_3.doc (editorialexpress.com)

Engel, Charles. 2002. Expenditure switching and exchange-rate policy. *NBER Eacroeconomics Annual, 17*, 231–272.

Gopinath, Gita, Boz, Emine, Casas, Camila, Díez, Federico J., Gourinchas, Pierre-Olivier, & Plagborg-Møller, Mikkel. 2020. Dominant currency paradigm. *American Economic Review, 110*(3), 677–719.

Hart, Oliver D., & Kreps, David M. 1986. Price destabilizing speculation. *Journal of Political Economy, 94*(5), 927–952.

Husain, Aasim M., Mody, Ashoka, & Rogoff, Kenneth S. 2005.Exchange rate regime durability and performance in developing versus advanced economies. *Journal of Monetary Economics, 52*(1), 35–64.

Ilzetzki, Ethan, Reinhart, Carmen M., & Rogoff, Kenneth S.2011.The country chronologies and background material to exchange rate arrangements into the 21st century: Will the anchor currency hold? Mimeo, NBER, working paper in 2017, No. 23135.

International Monetary Fund (IMF). 2007. *Assessing underlying vulnerabilities and crisis risks in emerging market countries – a new approach.*

International Monetary Fund (IMF). 2017. *Assessing country risk – selected approaches. Reference note.*

International Monetary Fund (IMF). 2019a. *Arab Republic of Egypt, fifth review under the extended arrangement under the extended fund facility.* www.imf.org/en/Publications/CR/Issues/2019/10/10/Arab-Republic-of-Egypt-Fifth-Review-Under-the-Extended-Arrangement-Under-the-Extended-Fund-48731, IMF Country report, No. 19/311

International Monetary Fund (IMF). 2019b. *Argentina, fourth review under the stand-by arrangement and request for modification of performance criteria, and financing assurances review.* www.imf.org/en/Publications/CR/Issues/2019/07/15/Argentina-Fourth-Review-under-the-Stand-By-Arrangement-Request-for-Waivers-of-Applicability-47116. IMF Country Report, No. 19/232.

International Monetary Fund (IMF). 2019c. *Hands-on workshop: systemic risk analysis in bilateral surveillance using SPR's SysRisk Tracker.*

International Monetary Fund (IMF). 2019d. *Pakistan, first review under the extended credit facility arrangement and request for modification of performance criteria*, www.imf.org/en/Publications/CR/Issues/2019/12/20/ Pakistan-First-Review-Under-the-Extended-Arrangement-Under-the-Extended-Fund-Facility-and-48899, IMF Country report, No. 19/380.

International Monetary Fund (IMF). 2020. *Fiscal monitor: Policies to support people during the pandemic*, ch. 3.

Jin, Zhongxia. 1995. On the reform of China's real exchange rate management. *Economic Research* (in Chinese), No. 3, pp. 63–71.

Jin, Zhongxia. 1996. On the equilibrium exchange rate formation mechanism in the transition period. *Economic Research* (in Chinese), No. 3, pp. 27–33.

Jin, Zhongxia. 2000a. International monetary system reform and China's choice. *World Economy* (in Chinese), No. 3, pp. 66–67.

Jin, Zhongxia. 2000b. The interactive relationship between China's exchange rate, interest rate and balance of payments: 1981–1999. *World Economy* (in Chinese), No. 9, pp. 19–24.

Jin, Zhongxia, & Hao, Chen. 2009. Analysis of the exchange rate of major currencies using interest rate parity theory. *Journal of Financial Research* (in Chinese), No. 8, pp. 92–110.

Jin, Zhongxia, & Hao, Chen. 2012.The realization form of interest rate parity theory in China. *Journal of Financial Research* (in Chinese), No. 7, pp. 63–67.

Jin, Zhongxia, & Hao, Hong. 2013. Equilibrium interest rate formation mechanism under open economic conditions: An explanation of the law of interest rate change in China Based on dynamic stochastic general equilibrium model (DSGE). *Journal of Financial Research* (in Chinese), No.7, pp. 46–60.

Jin, Zhongxia, & Hao, Hong. 2015. The coordination of interest rate policy and exchange rate policy in the international monetary environment. *Economic Research Journal* (in Chinese), No. 5, pp. 35–47.

Jin, Zhongxia, Hao, Hong, & Hongjin, Li. 2013. The impact of interest rate marketization on the effectiveness of monetary policy and economic structural adjustment. *Economic Research* (in Chinese), No. 4, pp. 69–82.

Kohlscheen, Emanuel, & Andrade, Sandro C. 2014. Official FX interventions through derivatives. *Journal of International Money and Finance*, *47*, 202–216.

Krüger, Malte. 1996. Speculation, hedging and intermediation in the foreign exchange market (No. 9606). SSRN: https://ssrn.com/abstract=1123426

Krugman, Paul. 1989.The case for stabilizing exchange rates. *Oxford Review of Economic Policy*, *5*(3), 61–72.

Krugman, Paul, & Taylor, Lance. 1978. Contractionary effects of devaluation. *Journal of International Economics*, *8*(3), 445–456.

Mendoza, Enrique G. 2010. Sudden stops, financial crises, and leverage. *American Economic Review, 100*(5), 1941–1966.

Mendoza, Enrique G., & Smith, Katherine A. 2006. Quantitative implications of a debt-deflation theory of sudden stops and asset prices. *Journal of International Economics*, *70*(1), 82–114.

Obstfeld, Maurice. 2017. Assessing global imbalances: The nuts and bolts. IMF blog. https://blogs.imf.org/2017/06/26/assessing-global-imbalances-the-nuts-and-bolts/

Reinhart, Carmen, & Calvo, Guillermo. 2002. Fear of floating. MPRA Paper,14000, University Library of Munich, Germany.

Rodrik, D. 2008. The real exchange rate and economic growth. *Brookings Papers on Economic Activity, 2008*(2), 365–412.

Rogoff, Kenneth. 2002. Dornbusch's overshooting model after twenty-five years. IMF Working Paper, No. 02/39.

Sergio, D. 2007. Does foreign exchange intervention remove overshooting? Working Paper. http://www.angelfire.com/id/SergioDaSilva/does.pdf

3 Further Developing the FX Derivatives Market and Allowing for a More Market-Based Regulatory Approach in China

International experiences suggest that it is crucial for a country to establish a FX derivatives market with sufficient depth and liquidity in order to successfully move toward a floating exchange rate regime while ensuring economic and financial stability. Although China has made great strides in developing its FX derivatives market in recent years, it still lacks an onshore FX futures market, which typically forms a critical component of a well-functioning multilayered FX market. Therefore, the FX derivatives market in China needs to be further developed in order to fully support a floating exchange rate.

While an over-the-counter (OTC) FX derivatives market already exists in China, it lacks a FX futures market, which is of paramount importance for serving a wider range of market participants such as SMEs and retail traders. Compared with the OTC market, the futures market boasts many advantages, such as standardized and low-cost products, a centralized market with greater transparency, lower credit risk, and more effective supervision. These advantages will help serve the hedging needs of broader market participants, which can, in turn, help reduce exchange rate fluctuations in the spot market.

It is worth mentioning that the FX futures market we allude to refers to the essential characteristics of the futures market, namely, high levels of standardization, low access barriers, greater transparency, and strong oversight. As to which specific platform should be used for FX futures markets, countries should be given the flexibility to make their specific choices. In China, the FX futures market can be established through either the interbank market or the exchange-traded market, which will be discussed later in this chapter.

DOI: 10.4324/9781003305668-3

Why Is a Foreign Exchange Futures Market Needed?

International experience has demonstrated the need to establish a FX futures market for both developed countries and developing countries in the course of advancing toward a floating exchange rate regime. FX futures markets were first established in developed countries such as the United States, the United Kingdom, and Japan. In 1971, Milton Friedman offered support for developing a US-based currency futures market in a short article that arguably established the intellectual foundation for a FX futures market. Friedman summarized the key rationales for developing an onshore FX futures market in the US: promoting foreign trade and investment, strengthening the US financial services industry, reducing the volatility of cross-border capital flows, and facilitating monetary policy implementation.

For major developing markets, the transition toward a more flexible exchange rate was often accompanied by the rapid development of the FX futures market. Take Brazil, for example. In January 1999, the Brazilian real was floated against the backdrop of continued depreciation pressure. The abandonment of the crawling peg led to sustained growth momentum in FX futures trading, with the trading volume growing tenfold between 1999 and 2008. Similarly in India, FX derivatives trading expanded rapidly alongside financial liberalization. Although trading in India's FX derivatives market was negligible before 1995, trading volume started to grow rapidly after the rupee's exchange rate became more flexible in 1995. In particular, the introduction of the onshore FX futures market had an impressive debut and has shown robust growth since its inception, with the annual turnover of exchange-traded options and futures rising sharply from INR 3.11 trillion in 2008–09 all the way to INR 98.96 trillion in 2011–12.

Although the OTCFX derivatives market in China has supported FX hedging for decades, the establishment of a FX futures market is urgently needed to encourage a broader range of market participants with hedging needs. At present, China's OTC FX derivatives market is mainly an interbank market offering tailor-made products to large companies and institutional clients. Notwithstanding the flexibility and diversity that the OTC market offers, its high transaction cost has prevented retail clients and SMEs from participating in the market. In recent years, the OTC market has started to tap electronic trading platforms and offer online products to help lower transaction costs for SMEs, yet problems such as high approval costs, nontransparent quotations, incomplete information coverage of clients, and a lack of centralized information still exist. Compared with the OTC market, the futures market – even with its relatively small size – has many advantages.

First, the onshore FX futures market will likely become the single largest centralized FX trading platform, thereby effectively strengthening price discovery and improving market liquidity. Despite the size of the OTC market, it is typically fragmented, with scattered bilateral transactions that are not conducive to price discovery. In addition, bilateral transactions depend heavily on bilateral credit and, thus, are suitable for more developed countries with sound credit systems. In contrast, an onshore FX futures market can serve as the single largest centralized trading platform to facilitate price discovery, improve market transparency, and reduce credit constraints. International experiences suggest that the FX futures market has an advantage in offering short-term financial products, whereas the OTC market does better in offering long-term financial products. In this regard, the FX futures market serves as an important complement to the OTC market.

Second, the onshore FX futures market can provide firms, especially SMEs, with low-cost tools to hedge exchange rate risks. Currently, China's FX derivatives coverage ratio, that is, the ratio between FX derivatives trading and international trade, is low compared with other emerging market countries, in part due to high hedging costs for firms, especially SMEs. The interbank OTC market mainly provides customized products that cater to large firms and institutional clients, with little incentive for banks to provide better priced products for SMEs due to lack of competition. In contrast, the FX futures market treats each type of market participant equally by providing them with standardized and low-cost hedging tools. In recent years, private enterprises dominated by SMEs have accounted for more than half of China's total exports. Hence, the FX risk management of SMEs has important macroeconomic implications for China's external risk exposure.

Third, the onshore FX futures market can compete effectively with the offshore market to resolve regulatory challenges associated with an oversized offshore market. In recent years, offshore RMB futures trading has grown rapidly, with daily trading volume exceeding USD 4 billion.[1] As demonstrated by international experiences, an oversized offshore market may bring about regulatory challenges such as increased volatility of cross-border capital flows, weakened capital flow management, and decreased domestic pricing power. The spillover effects from the offshore to the onshore market are most disruptive when the offshore market is large relative to the onshore market and when capital account restrictions create onshore–offshore pricing gaps. In addition, the absence of a central clearing platform may make a fragmented offshore market less effective in price discovery while increasing vulnerability to panics and liquidity squeezes when market conditions tighten. The development of a deep and highly liquid onshore market helps reduce the systemic risks and regulatory difficulties associated with offshore market volatility.

That said, it should be clarified that the intention of developing an onshore FX futures market is not to compete for FX "pricing power" through administrative means. Instead, the aim is to cultivate and develop a deep exchange rate market with flexible and transparent prices that can accurately reflect market supply and demand. The pricing power is not controlled by administrative factors, but is rather determined by market participants. The market with de facto pricing power must be the one where price can truly reflect supply and demand.

Fourth, the establishment of the onshore FX futures market is in line with the G20's OTC derivatives reform agenda and will help strengthen the authorities' regulatory capacity in the FX market. Prudential regulation is essential to ensure the stability and sustainability of the FX derivatives market. The 2008 financial crisis demonstrated the vulnerabilities of the OTC derivatives market, such as the excessive accumulation of counterparty risk, a lack of transparency, and a range of operational deficiencies. In contrast, the FX futures market will ensure that most transactions are centrally settled, which will, in turn, effectively reduce the exposure of private sector counterparties, thereby mitigating macro-financial risks.

Finally, the establishment of onshore FX futures markets will enable cross-border investors to better manage FX risk. Compared with the offshore FX futures market, the onshore FX futures market can better meet the hedging needs of international investors who invest in China's onshore bond and stock markets. In addition, the establishment of onshore FX futures markets will also help decrease cross-border capital flows, since the establishment of an onshore market will allow hedging activities to transfer to and from accounts within China, while the use of the offshore futures market by domestic traders and investors would produce more cross-border capital flows.

Empirical Study: "Stabilizer" or "Risk Amplifier"

Despite the benefits of establishing an FX futures market, some policy makers have concerns about "speculative activities" by derivatives traders that may increase the volatility of underlying exchange rates. On the theoretical front, there exist two opposing views in the literature regarding the impact of FX derivatives trading in the underlying spot markets. Some argue that the existence of derivatives markets helps stabilize exchange rates by reducing their fluctuations. A key feature of the derivatives market is the diversity of market participants, which includes not only hedgers but also speculators. In an efficient FX market, well-informed speculators make a profit by buying low and selling high, thereby helping to stabilize the market by reducing the impact of one-way transactions (Friedman, 1953). When the demand for liquidity changes, the speculators, expecting that the exchange rate will eventually return to equilibrium, can take reverse positions that serve to reduce exchange rate fluctuations (Carlson and Osler, 2000). In addition, speculative activity serves to deepen the market and will make it easier for market participants to hedge at low costs (Friedman, 1953; Powers, 1970; Danthine, 1978; Bray, 1981; Kyle, 1985). The futures market can also enhance price discovery in the FX market and increase the amount of information reflected in prices (Stoll and Whaley, 1988).

Other studies, however, argue that high leverage and speculation in the derivatives market may magnify risks in the spot market. Paul Krugman (1989) pointed out that some speculators are reluctant to assess whether the exchange rate is in line with long-term fundamentals and will instead try to predict and speculate on the views of other investors, which can lead to higher market volatility. At the same time, the high leverage and speculative nature of the derivatives market will inevitably attract some uninformed speculators who do not always "buy low and sell high", thereby reducing the information content of prices while increasing spot market volatility (Hart and Kreps, 1986; Stein, 1987).

Overall, the theoretical literature is inconclusive about the impact of the derivatives market on the spot market. Likewise, empirical research on this issue also produces no conclusive results. As Lee and Ohk (1992) pointed out, the impact of the derivatives market on the volatility of the spot market differs from country to country – not only because of the different structure of individual markets, but also due to country-specific conditions and the regulatory practices in each country. Clifton (1985) observed an increase in volatility in the currency spot market after the introduction of futures by using data from Chicago's International Monetary Market. Chatrath et al. (1996) and Shastri et al. (1996) studied the impact of the introduction of futures trading on the volatility in the spot rates of the British pound, Canadian dollar, Japanese yen, Swiss franc, and deutsche mark, but the two papers had opposite findings. Whereas the former found that currency futures trading increased the volatility of exchange rates, the latter found that the volatility of exchange rates decreased following the introduction of FX derivatives.

Despite the diverse views in the theoretical literature, it is standard practice for a market to allow speculation as it is practically impossible to distinguish between "hedgers" with speculative intention and "speculators". The impact of speculation mainly hinges on specific conditions and regulatory practices in each country.

Empirical studies have examined different countries, but most have focused on developed countries. A few papers investigate the effects of introducing FX futures markets in emerging economies (Jochum and Kodres, 1998; Oduncu, 2011; Nath and Pacheco, 2018), but they are mostly country-specific rather than cross-country studies. Unlike most existing literature analyzing the impact of the derivatives market on developed countries, we focus on emerging markets by studying whether the establishment of FX futures markets among BRICS (Brazil, Russia, India, China, and South Africa) countries increases the volatility of the underlying spot FX markets. Currently, China still requires documentation of underlying exposure for derivatives traders, which was also the case in other emerging market economies, such as India and South Africa before they established FX futures markets. In this regard, the experiences of developing countries are more relevant for China than those of developed countries.

Data and methodology: The historical time series of exchange rates are from Bloomberg. We use the daily closing values for the following currency pairs: USDINR, USDRUB, and USDZAR.[2] Our focus is on examining how exchange rate volatility changes before and after the introduction of a FX futures market. To "identify" the introduction of the futures market, it is critical to choose an appropriate cutoff date that separates episodes with and without FX futures trading. As the futures markets in some countries experienced very low trading volume immediately after their introduction and only took off several years later, we have chosen a cutoff date that marks the beginning of a stable rise in currency futures trading. Accordingly, the cutoff dates chosen for India, Russia, and South Africa are January 2009, January 2006, and January 2008, respectively. Both the Pre-cutoff-period (Pre-period) and the Post-cutoff-period (Post-period) are set to two years before and after the cutoff date.[3] Two years should be long enough to capture the effects of introducing currency futures, whereas periods longer than two years may incorporate more factors than the futures markets and be noisier.

The daily rate of return (of the local currency) is calculated by taking the natural logarithm of the ratio of the present day's index level with the previous day's index level. Before estimating the models, the unit root properties of each series are tested using ADF methods.

The volatility of the spot rate is modeled using the GARCH model for both the Pre-period and Post-period. GARCH models explain variance by two distributed lags. The first one, representing the autoregressive conditional heteroskedasticity (ARCH) effect, uses past squared residuals to capture news about volatility from the previous period, measured as the lag of the squared residuals from the mean equation. The second one is the lagged values of the variance itself and captures the long-term effect of old news, representing the GARCH effect. The specification is shown in Equation (1) and Equation (2).

$$y_t = v_t + \varepsilon_t \ldots (1)$$

$$\sigma_t^2 = \alpha_0 + \alpha_1 \varepsilon_{t-1}^2 + \beta \sigma_{t-1}^2 \ldots (2)$$

Parameter constraints:

$\alpha_0 > 0$

$\alpha_1 > 0$

$\beta \geq 0$

$\alpha_1 + \beta < 1,$

where y_t represents the daily return series of the closing spot rate, v_t is the intercept term, and ε_t is the residual term of the mean model. α_0 is the constant term of the conditionally heteroskedastic variance equation, ε_{t-1}^2 is the lagged squared error, and α_1 (ARCH coefficient) shows the impact of current news on volatility. σ_{t-1}^2 is the lagged conditional variance, and β represents the impact of old news on volatility, indicating the persistence of past information (the GARCH effect). Parameters α_0, α_1, and β should be greater than zero for the conditional variance to be non-negative. In order to ensure that the conditional variance is covariance stationary, α_1 plus β should be smaller than one. The Lagrange multiplier (LM) test was conducted to determine the presence of the ARCH effect of the residuals.

Empirical Results and Main Findings

We conducted empirical studies and robustness checks for India, Russia, and South Africa, the details of which may be found in Appendix 1. Our empirical results show that the establishment of the FX futures market did not increase the volatility of the spot market; on the contrary, it is empirically associated with a decrease in volatility in some cases. One possible reason is that the more diversified pool of participants, including speculators, helps the exchange rate return to its equilibrium faster by "buying low and selling high", thereby generating a stabilizing effect on the market. The empirical finding is more apparent when we exclude the financial crisis period from the sample to better isolate the impact of the FX futures market. This implies that, for emerging market countries, the FX futures market acts more like a market stabilizer rather than a volatility amplifier.

Regulatory Design: Moving toward a More Market-Based Approach

In order for the FX futures market to become a stabilizer, it is essential to ensure the stability of the FX derivatives market through prudential regulation. China currently requires documentation of underlying exposure for derivatives traders, a regulatory approach that is not in line with international practice and can impede the development of China's derivatives markets. Hence, the near-term priorities for China include gradually phasing out the current requirement of underlying exposure and allowing for a more market-based approach to regulating market risks. For countries that have phased out the requirement of underlying exposure, regulators mainly resort to market-based regulatory measures such as margin requirement (leverage ratio), limitations on margins, position limits, and daily price bands to manage the risks of the futures market. Net settlement and local currency settlement can also minimize possible risks in the FX futures market.

With the establishment of the FX futures market, the current requirement of underlying exposure should be gradually phased out. The requirement of underlying exposure in China once played an active role in promptly informing regulators of the trade-based FX demand in the real sector. However, such a requirement has become increasingly counterproductive to market development in recent years given increasing currency flexibility and more diversified currency demand.

First, the requirement of underlying exposure may result in trading in a homogenized direction, thereby exacerbating pro-cyclical fluctuations in the FX market. As Friedman pointed out, although foreign payments are in balance over a long period (forward sales of currencies for hedging purposes just balance forward purchases for hedging purposes), there is nothing to ensure that such a balance will hold in the short term or for each foreign country separately. An active market needs speculators who are willing to take open positions as well as hedgers who have underlying exposure. Second, under the requirement of underlying exposure, the scale of onshore FX derivatives markets is limited by the size of cross-border trade and investment. The requirement constrains market liquidity and depth, and impedes the role of price discovery as well as the internationalization of the RMB. Third, such a requirement cannot meet the needs of the traders who hedge FX risks in a preemptive manner, because documentation of underlying exposure can only happen after trade and investment transactions actually take place. Fourth, this requirement will mask rather than eliminate speculation, as can be shown in the large-scale capital flight when the exchange rate is significantly overvalued and in excessive capital inflows when the exchange rate is significantly undervalued.

International experiences suggest that the establishment of the futures market can function as a starting point toward relaxing the requirement of underlying exposure. Take India as an example. Before the FX futures market was first established in 2008, the requirement of underlying exposure was in place, and market participants were only permitted to transact in the derivatives markets to hedge an existing underlying exposure. Prior to the establishment of the FX futures market, the Internal Working Group on Currency Futures at the Reserve Bank of India (RBI) determined that the requirement of underlying exposure could not remain valid under a futures regime, as futures by definition are meant to be used for both hedging and speculation. They recommended that the restrictions on trading purposes be modified, and that OTC market restrictions be removed in a phased manner.[4] In accordance with the suggestions of the Internal Working Group, the requirement of underlying exposure was relaxed with the establishment of the FX futures market. Indian institutions and individuals could enter the FX futures market for hedging or other purposes without providing supporting evidence unless the volume of transactions reached a certain amount. The establishment of the FX futures market marked an important step forward in the RBI's liberalization of the FX derivatives market.

Currently, most developed countries allow speculators to participate in the FX futures market without any requirement of underlying exposure. Only a few developing countries maintain such requirements for certain segmented submarkets. For countries without these requirements, regulators mainly take a market-based approach to manage risks, relying on tools such as leverage ratios, limitations on banks' financing, position limits, and daily price bands. Chinese regulators can similarly replace the current requirement of underlying exposure with market-based regulatory tools, which have proven to be broadly effective. To ensure compatibility with the existing FX regulatory framework, the FX futures market in China can be initially designed with local-currency denominated cash settlement to avoid conflict with the limit on individual FX purchasing.

Next, we discuss some possible options toward adopting a market-based approach to regulate the FX futures market.

Margin requirement (leverage ratio): The primary purpose of a margin requirement is to protect the counterparty against an abrupt change in prices; regulators can also use it as a tool to adjust participants' leverage ratios. Insufficient margin requirement may result in increased market risks, whereas excessive margin requirement may increase transaction costs and discourage trading. Cross-country data show that the margin requirements in emerging market economies lie within 5%–10%, which implies a leverage ratio of between 10 and 20 times. Hence, the initial margin requirement for China may be set at 5% (allowing 20 times leverage) for most customers and 10% (allowing ten times leverage) for specific customers with higher risk profiles. This ratio can be adjusted over time based on market conditions and should gradually decrease as the FX futures market becomes more mature. In most developed economies, the margin requirement is usually less than 5%. For example, the margin requirements of various USD/CNH Futures products in the CME group are between 1.5% and 2.4%; the margin requirement of USD/CNH Futures in the Hong Kong Stock Exchange is around 2%; and the margin requirement of USD/CNH Futures in the Singapore Exchange is about 1%. These examples can provide a useful reference for adjusting the margin requirement as the onshore FX futures market gradually matures over time.

Restrictions on margin/net financial assets: In addition to setting margin requirements, regulators could also place restrictions on the net financial assets of traders for the margin. Margins financed by borrowings should be prohibited to reduce systemic financial risks. The margin of individual and institutional traders can be capped at a certain percentage of their net financial assets, with the aim of balancing their needs for FX hedging and potential risks from margin loss. The percentage of margin to participants' net financial assets can be set at different levels corresponding to different scales of net financial assets and different degrees of trading orientation.

Position limits: To prevent market manipulation and overconcentrated positions, position limits on market participants may be implemented. For example, India sets the gross open position limits of clients and members at 6% and 15% of total open interests respectively. China could also set position limits, beyond which a warning would be triggered for different types of market participants. The position limits could be dynamically adjusted as market depth and liquidity increase.

Settlement: Cash settlements and physical delivery are two primary methods for settling a currency futures contract, each with its own advantages. Cash settlement is simpler and more convenient than physical delivery, while physical delivery can meet the actual currency needs of market participants. Cash settlement is more popular among speculators without currency conversion demands and, consequently, amplifies the liquidity of the derivatives market. Cash settlement is also more suitable for countries without full capital account convertibility as it circumvents transactions involving foreign currencies. In general, physical delivery-based FX futures have been popular in countries with full capital account convertibility, while countries without full convertibility prefer cash-settlement contracts.

Given the complications generated by delivery-based settlements and the fact that China's capital account is not fully convertible, cash settlement in the local currency is a better choice for China in the early stages of establishing a FX futures market. Cash settlement in the local currency can also help reduce risks and mitigate pressure on cross-border capital flows. International experiences suggest that the choice of settlement should be in line with a country's capital account opening process. As China advances toward capital account convertibility, the settlement method should also be adjusted accordingly.

Daily price bands: There are two opposing views on whether daily price bands should be set. Some believe that the price bands would impede the role of price discovery in the FX futures market; others argue that the price bands can curb irrational behavior and mitigate risks in times of market disorder. In practice, most developed and developing countries do not set daily price bands for their currency futures markets. India and Hungary are two of a handful of countries that set daily price bands.[5] Currently, most offshore RMB futures markets do not have daily price bands. As China's central bank has withdrawn from regular FXI, there is little need to impose daily price bands. An artificial price band may draw speculation and attacks, and may cause differences between onshore and offshore prices. Meanwhile, it should be clearly stated to the market participants that the central bank is an active member of the FX futures market and reserves the right to intervene when necessary. In fact, central banks worldwide have adopted a variety of interim measures to curb speculation and maintain financial stability in times of disorderly market conditions.[6]

Role of central banks and supervisory authorities: FX futures market oversight is a highly nuanced area and involves multiple regulatory bodies; as such, coordination among different regulatory agencies is indispensable. The nature of the FX futures market (i.e., financial derivatives with the exchange rate as the underlying asset) requires joint oversight by the central bank and the securities regulatory commission. Based on international practices, the central bank should be responsible for providing market access guidance, monitoring market participants' sources of financing, and dynamically setting trading parameters, such as participants' margin requirements and position limits. In addition, the central bank can directly participate in the FX futures market as an active member and can opt to intervene in times of disorderly market conditions. In addition, the securities regulatory commission is responsible for enforcing regulations and standards for market participants under its supervisory purview. Effective coordination across different regulatory bodies will play an important role in safeguarding the stability of the FX futures markets.

A well-functioning FX futures market also requires more widespread use of derivatives tools by market participants. Currently, China's usage of FX derivatives is still lower than its peers, partly due to inadequate adoption of "hedge accounting". Hedge accounting can help firms avoid large fluctuations in profits caused by the repeated adjustments of the value of financial derivatives. Widespread practice of such an accounting method can help mitigate enterprises' concerns about the volatility of financial derivatives and the ensuing financial losses that may hurt their competitiveness. To further encourage Chinese enterprises to adopt hedge accounting, regulators should educate enterprises and investors to have a risk-neutral perspective and focus on the core business instead of the profits and losses caused by financial derivatives. Enterprises and investors should be informed that financial derivatives can help the firms obtain stable returns and are financially neutral in the long run.

Choice of Platforms for Establishing an FX Futures Market in China

The discussion of FX futures markets in this chapter has focused on their essential characteristics – namely, high levels of standardization, low access barriers, greater transparency, and strong oversight. As for the question of which specific platform should be used for FX futures markets, countries should be granted the flexibility to make their own specific choice. In China, the FX futures market can be established through either the interbank market or the exchange-traded market. Each platform has its own advantages and disadvantages.

Although most FX futures markets worldwide have been established at an exchange, similar platforms may face significant challenges in China. Compared with the interbank market, the exchange has had decades of experience regulating margin trading and serving diversified market participants, including individuals, to encourage competition. However, the main problem with an exchange is the difficulty in boosting market liquidity quickly at the initial stage of the market. The onshore FX futures market will inevitably face fierce competition from the existing OTC market and offshore FX futures market given similarities in their products. It will be very difficult for the FX futures market to thrive or even survive if market liquidity is insufficient. Japan, Australia, and many European countries have experienced a thin or shrinking market right after the establishment of their futures markets. Given the relatively small size of the FX futures market,[7] insufficient liquidity may become a significant obstacle to China's efforts to establish an FX futures market. Therefore, the criteria for platform selection should prioritize liquidity and development considerations.

Accordingly, China could consider setting up an FX futures market based in the interbank market to avoid insufficient liquidity at the initial stage, given that commercial banks in China are the largest participants in the FX market. One major advantage of establishing an FX futures market based in the interbank market is the ability to fully mobilize banks' participation. Banks, with their vast customer resources, can help improve the liquidity of the futures market and market efficiency, preventing the FX futures market from failing at the outset. This design is also in line with the inclusive nature of the futures market in that it helps the forward market and the futures market to complement instead of compete with each other. Currently, interbank market participants are accustomed to making FX transactions, and the financial infrastructure in the interbank market is also advanced enough to facilitate the establishment of the market.

No matter which platform is used, it is critical to allow all types of market participants to access the market at its inception. All institutions and individuals with exchange rate exposure should have access to the FX futures market and should be regulated through a market-based approach. It should feature an electronic platform to encourage cross-boundary participation. The more diverse the market participants, the more valuable and informative the price. Commercial banks and other institutions should also be allowed to enter both the OTC market and the futures market as market makers and arbitrageurs to narrow the spread between the two markets.

Notes

1 Currently the largest two offshore RMB futures markets are the Singapore Exchange (SGX) and Hong Kong Exchanges and Clearing (HKEX), with average daily trading volume of USD 4.1 billion and 785 million respectively in May 2021.
2 Brazil is a special case. In 1987, Brazil established its FX futures market and the trading volume started to rise steadily in 1994. However, in 1994, Brazil also launched its official currency, the real. As a result, Brazil's FX fluctuations were more affected by changes in the exchange rate regime than by the establishment of the FX futures market. Therefore, Brazil is excluded from our sample.
3 In the literature, there are typically two different approaches to determining the sample periods. One is to choose a fixed period before and after the cutoff date for each country, while the other is to choose the same period for all countries no matter what their cutoff dates are. We take the first approach to capture more country-specific factors.
4 For instance, if corporations were to be required to disclose unhedged exposures and the results of hedging, there would no longer be a need to verify the existence of an underlying commercial transaction.
5 India sets different percentage limits for contracts with different durations, while the Budapest Stock Exchange in Hungary sets daily maximum volatility thresholds based on the absolute change of the exchange rate rather than on a certain percentage.
6 For example, during the 2011–2012 rupee crisis, the RBI adopted measures such as reducing position limits and curbing banks from arbitraging between the FX futures market and OTC market. In response to financial market volatility in March 2020, many countries temporarily intervened in the FX market or restricted short-selling.
7 According to the Chicago Mercantile Futures Exchange, the FX futures market only accounts for about 5%–10% of FX derivatives transactions.

References

Adrian, Tobias, & Shin, Hyun Song. 2014. Procyclical leverage and value-at-risk. *The Review of Financial Studies*, *27*(2), 373–403.
Bray, Margaret. 1981. Futures trading, rational expectations and the efficient market hypothesis. *Econometrica*, *49*, 575–596.
Carlson, John A., & Osler, Carol L. 2000. Rational speculators and exchange rate volatility. *European Economic Review*, *44*(2), 231–253.

Chatrath, Arjun, Ramchander, Sanjay, & Song, Frank. 1996. The role of futures trading activity in exchange rate volatility. *Journal of Futures Markets, 16,* 561–584.

Chicago Mercantile Exchange Group. 2017. *Clearing risk management and financial safeguards.* CME Group Report.

Clifton, Eric. 1985. The currency futures market and interbank FX trading. *Journal of Futures Markets, 5,* 375–384.

Danthine, Jean-Pierre. 1978. Information, futures prices and stabilizing speculation. *Journal of Economic Theory, 17,* 79–98.

Friedman, Milton. 1953. The case for flexible exchange rates. In *Essays in positive economics* (pp. 157–203). Chicago: University of Chicago Press.

Gopinath, Shyamala. 2010. Over-the-counter derivative markets in India—issues and perspectives. *Financial Stability Review,* No. 14, July.

Hart, Oliver D., & Kreps, David M. 1986. Price destabilizing speculation. *Journal of Political Economy, 94*(5), 927–952.

Jin, Zhongxia, Wang, Haobin, & Zhao, Yue. 2021. The macroeconomic impact of FX intervention: Some cross-country empirical findings. IMF Working Paper.

Jin, Zhongxia, Zhao, Yue, & Wang, Haobin. 2021. *RMB: From marketization to internationalization.* Beijing: China Financial Publishing House (in Chinese).

Jochum, Christian, & Kodres, Laura. 1998. Does the introduction of futures on emerging market currencies destabilize the underlying currencies? *IMF Staff Papers, 45*(3), 486–521.

José, Luiz Rossi. 2007. The use of currency derivatives by Brazilian companies: an empirical investigation. *Brazilian Review of Finance, Brazilian Society of Finance, 5*(2), 205–232.

Krüger, Malte. 1996. Speculation, hedging and intermediation in the FX market (No. 9606). SSRN: https://ssrn.com/abstract=1123426

Krugman, Paul. 1989. The case for stabilizing exchange rates. *Oxford Review of Economic Policy, 5*(3), 61–72.

Krugman, Paul, & Taylor, Lance. 1978. Contractionary effects of devaluation. *Journal of International Economics, 8*(3), 445–456.

Kyle, Albert. 1985. Continuous auction and insider trading. *Econometrica, 53,* 1315–1335.

Lee, Sang Bin, & Ohk, Ki Yool. 1992. Stock index futures listing and structural change in time-varying volatility. *The Journal of Futures Markets, 12,* 493–509.

Nath, Nath, & Pacheco, Manoel. 2018. Currency futures market in India: An empirical analysis of market efficiency and volatility. *Macroeconomics and Finance in Emerging Market Economies, 11*(1), 47–84.

Oduncu, Arif. 2011. The effects of currency futures trading on Turkish currency market. *Journal of BRSA Banking and Financial Markets, Banking Regulation and Supervision Agency, 5*(1), 97–109.

Powers, Mark. 1970. Does futures trading reduce price fluctuations in the cash markets?. *American Economic Review, 60,* 460–4.

Prakash, Anand. 2012. Major episodes of volatility in the Indian FX market in the last two decades (1993-2013): Central Bank's response. *Reserve Bank of India Occasional Papers, 33*(1 & 2). rbidocs.rbi.org.in

Reserve Bank of India. 2008. *Report of the internal working group on currency future.* rbidocs.rbi.org.in

Shastri, Kuldeep, Sultan, Jahangir, & Tandon, Kishore. 1996. The impact of the listing of options in the FX market. *Journal of International Money and Finance, 15,* 37–64.

Stein, Jeremy. 1987. Informational externalities and welfare reducing speculation. *Journal of Political Economy, 95,* 1123–1145.

Stoll, Hans R., & Whaley, Robert E. 1988 Volatility and futures: Message versus messenger. *Journal of Portfolio Management, 14*(2), 20–22.

4 Floating Exchange Rate and the Internationalization of the RMB

At the current development stage of the Chinese economy, a key symbol that would reflect substantive improvement in the RMB's internationalization is that RMB-denominated financial assets can be more widely held by international investors. This entails two preconditions: First, investors must at least believe that Chinese government bonds will not default; and second, investors believe that the RMB financial assets they hold can be conveniently converted into financial assets in other currencies, and in particular, with the freedom to sell and obtain foreign exchange. At present, China meets the first precondition, and is just beginning to meet the second, starting from a low level and on a limited basis. If investors at home and abroad were to choose between a stable and fixed RMB exchange rate and a convertible RMB, the latter would definitely be preferable.

A floating exchange rate regime can reduce one-sided appreciation or depreciation expectation, diminishing the incentives for RMB holders to seek one-time and unsustainable profits by relying on covered interest arbitrage under the current account. With a floating exchange rate, cross-border market players will use RMB primarily as a means of payment and seek to reduce currency mismatch, lower exchange rate volatility risk, and currency conversion cost, supporting the RMB to achieve inflow and outflow balance under the current account.

It is important to note, however, that if the use of the RMB is limited merely to the current account, the RMB can hardly become an internationalized currency. This is because in practice, importers and exporters cannot transact seamlessly, and will hence accumulate a certain amount of RMB balance. If the RMB balance can only be deposited in the bank to earn low interest, it will incur high opportunity cost for the holder and dampen the attractiveness of holding RMB. If this RMB balance could be invested in the Chinese financial market to generate investment returns, it would increase the overall attractiveness

DOI: 10.4324/9781003305668-4

of holding RMB. Fortunately, China has become the second-largest bond market and stock market in the world; both have the potential to become an attractive investment pool and anchorage for non-resident RMB holders.

With a free-floating RMB, well-established FX forward and futures markets, and the ability to keep money and external debt growth under control, China's capital market is ready to open up further gradually.

Liberalizing the Capital Market Further

As of end-2019, total foreign reserves held by central banks around the world amounted to approximately USD 11.8 trillion, of which the RMB accounted for 1.96%. We are not only a long way off when compared to the USD's 60.89% and the EUR's 20.54%, but are also behind the GBP's 4.62% and the JPY's 5.7%. If the share of RMB assets among total foreign reserves were to increase to 5%, foreign central banks would have to increase their RMB asset holdings by USD 360 billion, or a total of approximately RMB 2.5 trillion. If these assets were to be held in the form of bonds, the incremental amount of bonds held by foreign central banks would be equivalent to approximately 2.5% of the total market value of the Chinese bond market, and 6.6% of the total market value of government bonds.[1]

In fact, when the IMF included the RMB in the Special Drawing Right (SDR) basket of currencies, it took into account the level of development of China's real economy, trade, and finance, and eventually set the weight of the RMB in the SDR basket at 10.92%. If the share of RMB assets in the foreign reserves of central banks around the world were to increase to 10.92%, this suggests that foreign central banks would have to invest an additional RMB 7.4 trillion or so in the Chinese bond market, equivalent to 7.5% of the total value of the Chinese bond market, and 20% of the total market value of government bonds. China should seek to further increase the share of the RMB among international reserve currencies to a proportionate level through market-oriented exchange rate reforms and further capital market liberalization.

Gradual liberalization of the bond market

As of Q1 2020, China's interbank bond market amounted to approximately RMB 103 trillion, of which about RMB 2.4 trillion was held by foreign investors.[2] Hence to date, foreign investors can access the Chinese bond market via channels such as SDR agreements, Bond Connect, QFII, RQFII, as well as by investing in international market indices. Total foreign holdings account for just 2%–3% of the total market value of the bond market, not only lower than the levels in the US (25%), Japan (12%), and South Korea (6%),[3] but also lower than that in most emerging market countries (see Figures 4.1–4.3). China should first seek to increase the participation rate of foreign investors to the average level of emerging markets. Meanwhile, China should gradually guide foreign governments, financial institutions, and enterprises to raise funds by issuing RMB bonds in China.

Improving and liberalizing the RMB bond market further will not only serve to lower the cost of debt, reduce currency mismatch, and increase the stability of cross-border capital flows, but it is also an inevitable path to take as the RMB evolves into an international reserve currency. Although the size of China's bond market has become the second largest in the world, its openness, liquidity, and market depth are still incompatible with its market size. China should break the development bottlenecks in the RMB bond market on multiple fronts, including further easing market access; making it more convenient for foreign entities to issue panda bonds and invest in the interbank bond market; expanding the range of bond markets in which foreign investors can participate, such as bond buybacks and government bond futures; boosting the liquidity and trading efficiency of the bond market by improving the market maker system; increasing the types of investors; enhancing the mix of government bond maturities and reducing differences in tax rules, among others; developing interest rate and FX derivatives markets to improve the risk hedging ability of domestic and foreign investors; providing accounting, auditing, and legal systems that are internationally compatible; improving default settlement mechanisms; and dampening expectations about implicit guarantee, among others.

Gradual liberalization of the stock market

As of end-2019, the total market capitalization of China's stock market stood at RMB 59.29 trillion, of which RMB 2.1 trillion was held by foreign institutions and individuals. The share of foreign investors was a mere 3.5%, not only lower than developed economies such as the US (15%), Japan (30%), and South Korea (33%), but also lower than emerging market economies[4] such as Brazil (21%) (see Figure 4.4).

In recent years, numerous initiatives and measures have been carried out to liberalize China's capital market, but there has been limited substantive progress. Such initiatives included the launch of Shanghai Connect and Shenzhen Connect; reforms to the Qualified Foreign Institutional Investor (QFII) system, including the abolishment of QFII and RQFII investment quotas; and wider inclusion of China's A shares

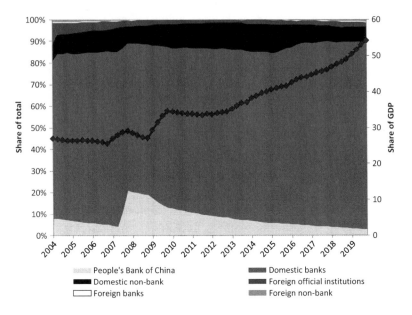

Figure 4.1 Breakdown of holders of China's central government bonds.

in international market indices. Nonetheless, the share of foreign ownership has not increased much. In fact, the specific criteria for judging whether China has made progress in its financial market liberalization is not in the number of open channels but in whether the share of foreign ownership rises. This ultimately depends on whether various implicit and explicit restrictions can be abolished, whether the liberalized institutional environment is comprehensive, whether exchange rates are flexible enough, and whether the inflow of capital will be restricted when it leaves the country, among many other factors.

The next step China should take is to leverage channels such as investors of international market indices, Shanghai- and Shenzhen-Hong Kong Connect Northbound, QFII, and RQFII to attract foreign investors to the secondary market and increase foreign ownership in the secondary market to the average level of emerging markets. Second, the international board should be permitted, as soon as possible, to attract not only quality companies from developed countries, creating an international blue-chip sector, but also high-growth enterprises along the "Belt and Road" as well as from other emerging market countries, creating an emerging market growth sector. This will not only allow China's onshore market to be able to facilitate global asset allocation denominated in the RMB, but also advance equity financing for "Belt

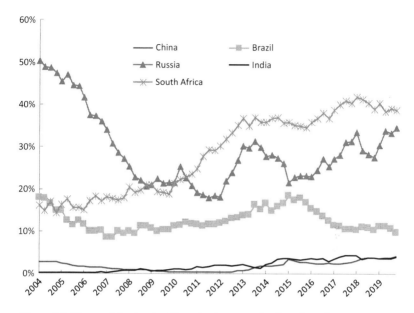

Figure 4.2 Share of foreign holdings in the sovereign bond market among
BRICS countries (% of total).

and Road" and other overseas investment projects, reducing China's
overreliance on bank financing for outbound investment projects that
leads to excessive leverage.

Third, China should regularly issue RMB government bonds and cen-
tral bank bills in the offshore market to provide RMB assets to inter-
national investors, and create an RMB government bond benchmark yield
curve in the offshore market. Overseas branches and affiliates of Chinese
funded banks should gradually offer to open RMB accounts for local
customers and provide them with wealth management services (see
Figure 4.5).

Supporting Measures for Liberalizing the Capital Market

First, the bond futures market and stock futures market should be further developed and improved so that a risk management mechanism
with market-driven measures may be established to address securities
price volatility. The combination of a securities risk management mechanism and an FX forward and futures market will provide cross-border
investors with a comprehensive set of cross-border risk management
toolkits.

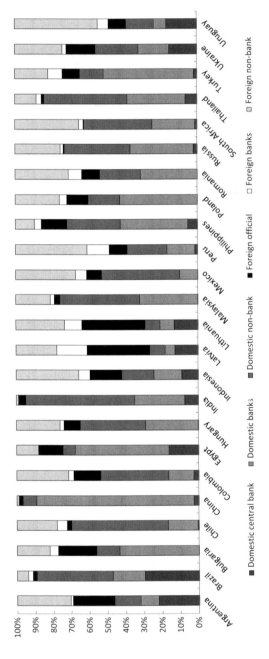

Figure 4.3 Breakdown of sovereign bond investors of emerging market countries (as of end-2019).

Sources: IMF, Arslanalp and Tsuda (2014 updated), and authors' estimates.

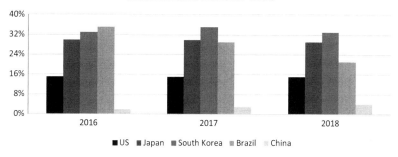

Figure 4.4 Share of equities held by foreign investors in major stock markets in recent years.

Source: *China's Balance of Payments Report 2018*, State Administration of Foreign Exchange.

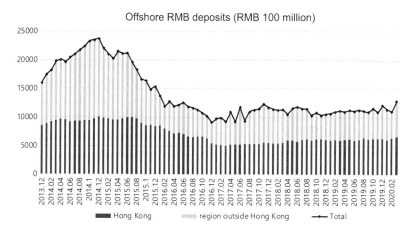

Figure 4.5 Offshore RMB deposits.

Source: PBOC, Hong Kong Monetary Authority.

Second, the central government should also establish a capital market stabilization fund that is of adequate and appropriate size comprising both FX and RMB. The FX in the fund will come from the accumulation of FX settlement when foreign investment flows into the capital market, and should not be used for other purposes. The RMB in the fund will be primarily guaranteed by the PBOC. Liquidity support will be provided in response to massive market sales and capital flight in the event of international financial market turmoil. However, even in times like this, the floating exchange rate regime must not be abandoned; the commitment to liberalize capital and financial account convertibility should not be compromised.

Third, bond ratings, accounting standards, and information disclosure standards should be aligned with international standards so as to minimize institutional costs for international investors who regularly switch between international markets and the Chinese market. China should also draw from international experiences and establish a legal system that supports bond and stock market liberalization, and that can effectively address issues such as debt default, restructuring, as well as corporate bankruptcies, so that international investors can have a standardized, transparent, and predictable market environment in China.

The opening up of investment channels should allow for two-way foreign capital flows while avoiding the "liberal inflows and restricted outflows" approach. The key reason for adopting the "liberal inflows and restricted outflows" approach is the fear of excessive exchange rate depreciation. However, the preceding chapters of this book have already addressed how excessive exchange rate depreciation may be prevented and exchange rate volatility managed under a floating exchange rate regime. For investors, outflow restrictions will force them to reduce or even abandon capital inflows. If a "liberal inflows and restricted outflows" stance is adopted even during good times, there will be few opportunities to liberalize outflows in the future. The outcome of asymmetrical liberalization is that liberalization of the Chinese capital market will remain de jure over a long period of time. Substantive progress will be difficult to achieve whether in terms of market development or in terms of RMB internationalization.

It is worth noting that under most circumstances (except in extreme situations), both RMB and FX capital that has flowed into China's liberalized markets should not be restricted from leaving the country through administrative measures. Rather, outflows should only be influenced through prices such as exchange rates and interest rates. So long as we adopt the aforementioned preventive arrangements in response to capital outflows, capital outflows will not be dramatic. Using administrative measures to restrict capital outflows causes more harm than good. It will not only dampen existing investors' confidence in regulatory credibility, but also fend off potential capital inflows over an extended period of time, ultimately affecting the international community's confidence in RMB assets.

Capital account convertibility should be carried out in stages, and in an orderly manner. First, certain excessively stringent controls over the current account may be gradually liberalized, such as the USD 50,000 annual quota for the individual resident's foreign currency purchase. Next, asymmetrically restricted items under the capital account (such as policies related to the "liberal inflows and restricted outflows" approach) may be liberalized further so as to ensure that FDI as well as portfolio inflows may flow out uninterrupted even during the cyclical reversals in global liquidity. This is not to encourage outflows, but rather to create greater confidence for capital inflows. Third, two-way liberalization of the bond and stock markets should continue to expand. Gradual liberalization is a process in which the RMB exchange rate adapts to and finds a new equilibrium.

Progressive capital account liberalization also means that certain restrictions will be retained over a particular period of time, such as the restriction on residents from exchanging the proceeds from a home sale to foreign currency and investing in overseas real estate. This is mainly because the house price-to-income ratio in China is higher than that in some developed countries. It should be noted, however, that China's house price-to-income ratio has been falling over the last decade, and the growth rate of the house price-to-income ratio is lower than most major countries (see Figure 4.6). Even if Chinese residents were to sell domestic housing and transfer the proceeds overseas, the resulting decline in house prices and exchange rate depreciation would curb home sales and demand for FX, allowing the price mechanism to automatically adjust and achieve supply-demand balance. In addition, we can spend ten years or so to control house price appreciation by regulating land supply and adopting other measures to keep house prices stable at current levels. As income rises over time, the house price-to-income ratio will decline. Capital outflow pressure as a result of exchanging proceeds from home sale to foreign currency will ease considerably.

Some believe that liberalizing capital account convertibility may lead to illicit capital flight, but these individuals only make up a very tiny part of the population. Hence, the majority's right to carry out normal cross-border transactions should not be compromised simply because of the presence of a small number of "illicit" individuals. In any case, capital controls should not be used as a means to investigate and restrict corrupt practices. Rather, the gate-keeping responsibility should fall on strengthening the domestic anti-corruption system, as well as enhancing international collaboration on anti-corruption, tax collection, and management.

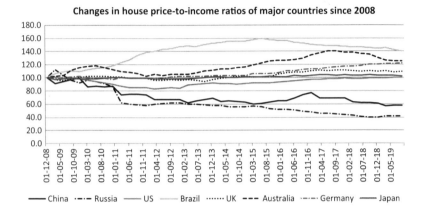

Figure 4.6 Changes in house price-to-income ratios of major countries
        since 2008.

Source: IMF.

International experience (see box below) shows that countries that
announce the implementation of a floating exchange rate regime and
capital and financial account convertibility put considerable weight
on defending their national commitment, and are extremely sensitive
to media reports and external commentaries on the implementation of
foreign exchange controls. The IMF has divided the management of
capital and financial accounts into market-oriented macroprudential
measures (MCM) and administrative-driven capital flow management
measures (CFMs). Both developed economies and emerging market
economies that commit to liberalization will react strongly if the IMF's
consultation report deems that CFMs have been adopted by a particular country, and the country will typically seek to have IMF staff
amend or downplay this.

**Box 4.1 Russia's policy choice under harsh international
sanctions**

Russia liberalized its capital and financial accounts in the
1990s, and adopted a corresponding monetary policy to keep
its exchange rate and goods price steady. However, intensifying
international financial market turmoil, sanctions by the West, and
collapsing international oil prices led to deteriorating BOP. The

Russian authorities abandoned the goal of exchange rate stability in November 2014, and allowed the ruble (RUB) to float freely without attempting to stabilize the exchange rate through capital controls. Russia did not adopt capital controls for the following reasons: First, with a liberalized current account, residents can circumvent control measures by other means, making controls inefficient, and even causing black market and the offshore exchange rates to deviate from official exchange rates, hurting the latter's credibility. Second, it could easily trigger legal issues pertaining to the violation of the provisions in Article VIII of the IMF's Articles of Agreement associated with current account convertibility and multiple currency practices. Third, as far as investors are concerned, capital controls are in fact a form of default. Once capital controls are implemented to an already liberalized current account, a capital-friendly environment that took years to build could be destroyed overnight, but recovering credibility will take a long time.

Conclusion

Compared with the development stage and openness of China's real economy, China's progress toward a floating exchange rate regime, capital market liberalization, and RMB internalization is lagging. There are legitimate reasons for such a situation, as industrial development typically advances ahead of financial development. However, if this situation remains stagnant for a long period of time, it will significantly impede the development of the real economy. Lagging financial development may even be fatal if the external environment deteriorates rapidly.

Capital account liberalization is neither a "black or white" nor a simple "yes or no" issue. In fact, the liberalization of China's capital account, particularly its capital market, is always ongoing, and has achieved some progress in terms of market size and volume. Compared with emerging market economies, however, the extent of China's capital market liberalization remains low currently. The existing state of the capital and financial accounts has not been able to meet the development needs of the real economy, and has hindered the pace of RMB internationalization, which will ultimately constrain our ability to respond effectively to the harsh challenges brought about by upheavals in the international environment.

Liberalizing the capital market too quickly or too slowly carries risks in either case. A particularly risky scenario that may arise is as follows: When confronted with major global changes and challenges, we are unable to achieve breakthroughs and further development through pro-active reforms and liberalization; rather, we passively seek stability out of fear of change, counting our gains and losses from a narrow perspective. We not only stop persisting in making market-oriented exchange rate reform and moving toward a more flexible exchange rate regime, but also spend our limited foreign reserves to fight a positional warfare with international capital for the sole purpose of maintaining a subjectively determined exchange rate level. Worse still, we even resort to suffocating market activity through FX controls, blocking the path toward RMB internationalization. Such a response will see history repeating itself, with greater controls causing FX to dwindle and the economy to shrink, ultimately leading to a dead end. Hence, to a certain extent, the choice of exchange rate regime is a key determinant of whether China can success-fully respond to dramatic global changes in the years to come.

Notes

1 Foreign reserves figures from the IMF COFER database; China's bond market data are from the PBOC.
2 China Central Depository & Clearing Co., Ltd., Shanghai Clearing House May 2020 data.
3 Source: *China's Balance of Payments Report 2018*, IMF, and BIS.
4 Data for total market capitalization of the stock markets from the Shenzhen and Shanghai stock exchanges; data for foreign institutional and individual holdings from the PBOC.

References

Arslanalp, Serkan & Tsuda, Takahiro 2014. Tracking Global Demand for Emerging Market Sovereign Debt, IMF Working Papers 2014/039, International Monetary Fund.

Jin, Zhongxia. 2012. China's Marshall Plan: Exploring China's foreign infrastructure investment strategy, *International Economic Review* (in Chinese), No. 6.

Jin, Zhongxia. 2013.China's capital and financial account opening and balance of payments dynamic balance, *International Economic Review* (in Chinese), No. 3, pp. 57–64.

Jin, Zhongxia, Zhao, Yue, & Wang, Haobin. 2021. *RMB: From marketization to internationalization*. Beijing: China Financial Publishing House (in Chinese).

State Administration of Foreign Exchange. 2018. *China's Balance of Payments Report*, Beijing.

Epilogue

We are at once delighted and anxious that this book is about to go to press. As researchers of China's economy and monetary policy, we are fortunate witnesses of significant changes, and the bearers of the responsibility and mission of our times. There have long been differing views about exchange rate policies and RMB internationalization. We too have not ceased to ponder over and explore the pros and cons of different policy choices. In the course of our research, we have had bouts of confusion and enlightenment, and have also experienced great joy from learning and pondering. As researchers, we strive to present our research findings in an objective, truthful, and impartial manner. We were presented with two options when selecting the research approach. One was to use given policy as an exogenous variable, and the other was to make the policy an object of our research. We picked the latter with a constructive attitude. We believe that this sort of research offers more value to decision makers and practitioners.

The research in this book is based on continued observation and study of exchange rate issues over the last few decades. It has benefited from important discussions conducted at the IMF, including those about exchange rate policies under multilateral and bilateral supervisions, as well as institutional views about capital flows. It has also benefited from recent country cases, particularly those pertaining to the experiences and lessons in exchange rate regimes, capital account management, and FX derivatives markets, including but not limited to the US, Japan, India, Russia, Brazil, Argentina, Egypt, and Pakistan. As regards technical issues associated with the FX derivatives market, we made special arrangements to hold discussions with experts from the Monetary and Capital Markets Department of the IMF, the CME Group, and the London FX market. We also visited and interviewed various FX market experts in Hong Kong SAR and mainland China.

This book contains the findings of a research project of the China Finance 40 Forum (CF40). Relevant experts and scholars as well as financial regulators gave their opinions and feedback on some preliminary conclusions of this book in August 2019. In the course of subsequent amendments and extensions, we also benefited from feedback and questions from relevant experts and policy makers. Prior to submission for CF40 review, we also sought the opinions of a number of senior experts and policy makers who were involved in the formulation of exchange rate policies since the early 1990s. Their opinions were very encouraging and enhanced our understanding of the challenges associated with and the significance of further promoting market-oriented reforms for the RMB exchange rate as well as financial market liberalization. CF40 conducted an interim review of this report in August 2020, which was then successfully concluded in November 2020.

We would like to take this opportunity to thank the various anonymous senior experts and leaders who once worked at or are still working at the PBOC and Ministry of Finance for their forbearance, encouragement, and critical advice. We would also like to thank CF40 for their support and for providing an excellent discussion and opinion exchange platform, especially CF40's Secretary-General Wang Haiming for his support and understanding. We would like to express our gratitude to Professor Li Yining at Peking University; Dr. Zhang Xiaohui, at Tsinghua PBC School of Finance; Dr. Yu Yongding at Chinese Academy of Social Sciences; Dr. Wang Chunying at the State Administration of Foreign Exchange; Dr. Huang Yiping at the National School of Development, Peking University; Dr. Wei Shangjin at Columbia Business School; and Dr. Gao Shanwen at Essence Securities for their valuable advice, encouragement, and support for the publication of this book. We would also like to acknowledge with gratitude our many colleagues such as Sun Guofeng, Zhu Jun, Guo Kai, and Shi Liya, among others, for their comments. We would like to thank Dr. Zhou Jianping, Kelly Eckhold, Asad Qureshi, and Christian Saborowski, economists with the IMF; Leo Melamed, Derek Sammann and Paul Houston of the CME Group; Zhang Xiaogang at China Financial Futures Exchange; Xiao Ting at Bank of Communications; and Hou Fei and Zhang Zhen at Bank of China for their professional and valuable views and advice. We are grateful to Dr. Xie Peichu, economist with the IMF, for his advice at the preliminary analysis of this project on the specific empirical analysis methodology, as well as to Dr. Zhu Junjun at China Europe International Exchange Ag (CEINEX) for his valuable contribution and advice. When we acknowledge our gratitude to these experts, we do not emphasize their duties and titles so as to highlight the research nature of this book.

We have conscientiously studied and analyzed the opinions of all parties, and taken them into consideration to the greatest extent possible, but have taken care to maintain the independence of our views. In the original research project, Sections 3 and 4 of Chapter 4 contained discussions on RMB internationalization in the context of COVID-19 and its impact on exchange rates. They were either hypothetical exploration or involved technical issues pertaining to execution, and were excluded from this book.

Elsewhere, we would like to thank research assistants Jin Shuhan, He Xinyi, Alena Zhang, Chen Xinyu, and Wu Liyang for compiling information and collecting data. We would also like to express our gratitude to Jin Shiwei at the Secretariat and Su Xianghui and Shao Suya at the Editorial Department of CF40, for their meticulous assistance during the course of preparing and publishing this book.

Last but not least, we would like to express the deepest gratitude to and longing for our family members. For a long period of time, most of our spare time was spent on work and research, and we sacrificed too many wonderful moments with them. Some have had to endure enormous pain at the deaths of their loved ones during COVID-19. We can only work harder and live better to console and repay our families.

At the time this book was completed, COVID-19 was still wreaking havoc worldwide. While inflicting pain on the human race, the virus is making profound changes to the international landscape and nurturing new opportunities. From marketization to internationalization, the RMB's journey is long and arduous, but it is moving in the right direction.

Confronted with a complex and vast epochal topic, the views contained in the book may have some narrow perspectives. The authors take full responsibility for any and all biases, omissions, and fallacies that exist herein. This is an effort to start a discussion. We welcome all comments and criticisms, and will continue to carry out research and discussions.

Appendix 1: Empirical Results and Robustness Checks
India, Russia, and South Africa

India

Table A1.1 presents the descriptive statistics of the daily returns over the Pre-period and Post-period. Table A1.2 shows the ADF test of the stationarity. The values of the t-statistics of USDINR during all the periods are statistically significant at the 1% significance level. Thus, this test confirms that all series under consideration are stationary.

The LM test for no ARCH effect of exchange rate returns is statistically significant with a zero probability, implying that there is a significant ARCH effect in exchange rate returns. The presence of heteroskedasticity in the exchange rate series shows the importance of using the ARCH family of models to study volatility.

Table A1.3 lists the α_1 and and β_1 coefficients coefficients of the GARCH (1,1) model, both of which are statistically significant at 1%, suggesting that the volatility of y_t is affected by recent information as

Table A1.1 Descriptive statistics USDINR

Variable	Obs	Mean	Std. Dev.	Min	Max
Pre	507	–0.0001923	0.0047907	–0.024074	0.0189109
Post	485	0.0001808	0.0053458	–0.0170301	0.0302912

Table A1.2 ADF test statistics value for USDINR

	Test Statistic	1% Critical Value	15% Critical Value	10% Critical Value	No. Obs	P value
Pre	–14.669	–3.458	–2.880	–2.570	507	0.0000
Post	–16.165	–3.460	–2.880	–2.570	485	0.0000

Table A1.3 GARCH (1,1) analysis for India

	Intercept (α_0)	ARCH (α_1)	GARCH (β_1)	$\alpha_1+\beta_1$
Pre-Derivative	5.40e-07	0.1595126	0.8292628	0.9887754
P value	0.000	0.000	0.000	0.000
Post-Derivative	3.08e-06	0.1259465	0.7386511	0.8645976
P value	0.000	0.000	0.000	0.000

well as past information. We found that, in comparison with the Pre-period, both the recent information and the past information caused less volatility in the Post-period. We also examined the level of volatility in the Indian currency market using the unconditional variance calculated as the ratio of α_0 to the difference between 1 and the sum of α_1 and β as follows:

$$\text{Var}\varepsilon_t = \frac{\alpha_0}{1-\left(\alpha_1 + \beta_1\right)}...(3)$$

The unconditional volatility of the GARCH process decreased from 0.00004810862 in the Pre-period to 0.00002274701 in the Post-period. These results show that the persistence of volatility decreased in the Post-period. The argument for the destabilizing effects of the currency futures markets is not supported in India's case.

Russia

As with India's case, we list the statistical summary and the results of the ADF test for Russia in Table A1.4. The table shows that all the series under consideration are stationary. Based on the results of the LM test shown in Table A1.5, the ARCH effect also exists in the exchange rate returns.

Table A1.6 lists the α_1 and β coefficients of the GARCH (1,1) model, both of which are statistically significant at 1%, suggesting that the volatility of y_t is affected by recent information as well as past information. However, unlike India's case, the ARCH coefficient decreases while the GARCH coefficient increases. The sum of α_1 and β remains approximately unchanged. We then calculate the unconditional variance by dividing α_0 by the difference between 1 and the sum of α_1 and β. With the introduction of the currency futures market, the unconditional variance decreased from 0.00000546285

Table A1.4 Descriptive statistics USDRUB

Variable	Obs	Mean	Std. Dev.	Min	Max
Pre	522	0.0000331	0.0019555	−0.006682	0.006992
Post	521	0.0002986	0.0021288	−0.0073153	0.0098162

Table A1.5 ADF test statistics value for USDRUB

	Test 1% Statistic	Critical 5% Value	Critical 10% Value	Critical Value	No. Obs	P value
Pre .	−21.517	−3.430	−2.860	−2.570	520	0.0000
Post	−22.323	−3.430	−2.860	−2.570	520	0.0000

Table A1.6 GARCH (1,1) analysis for Russia

	Intercept (α_0)	ARCH (α_1)	GARCH (β_1)	$\alpha_1 + \beta_1$
Pre-Derivative	8.60e-08	0.1023693	0.881888	0.9842581
P value	0.000	0.000	0.000	0.000
Post-Derivative	4.71e-08	0.0329523	0.9573649	0.9968879
P value	0.281	0.017	0.000	0.000

to 0.0000048643. These results indicate that the change in the overall volatility in the Post-period, if any, is probably downward, which again is at odds with the concerns about the destabilizing effects of currency futures markets.

South Africa

Similarly, the time series of exchange returns in South Africa also shows stationarity and the existence of the ARCH effect, as seen in Tables A1.7 and A1.8.

Table A1.9 lists the α_1 and β coefficients of the GARCH (1,1) model, both of which are statistically significant at 1%. The ARCH coefficients and GARCH coefficients go in opposite directions: The ARCH coefficients increased whereas the GARCH coefficients decreased, suggesting that the volatility coming from the new information increased, while the volatility from the persistent old information decreased. Overall, the unconditional variance of the returns increased.

Table A1.7 Descriptive statistics USDZAR

Variable	Obs	Mean	Std. Dev.	Min	Max
Pre	521	−0.0001554	0.0096418	−0.032557	0.0277545
Post	523	−0.0001437	0.0163603	−0.154965	
				0.0662992	

Table A1.8 ADF test statistics value for USDZAR

	Test 1% Statistic	Critical 5% Value	Critical 10% Value	Critical Value	No. Obs	P value
Pre	−23.344	−3.430	−2.860	−2.570	520	0.0000
Post	−23.688	−3.430	−2.860	−2.570	520	0.0000

Table A1.9 GARCH (1,1) analysis for South Africa

	Intercept (α_0)	ARCH (α_1)	GARCH (β_1)	$\alpha_1 + \beta_1$
Pre-Derivative	4.01e-06	0.0322642	0.9247918	0.957056
P value	0.250	0.098	0.000	0.098
Post-Derivative	5.00e-06	0.1492664	0.8454004	0.9946668
P value	0.164	0.000	0.000	0.000

The trading volume of currency futures in South Africa started to rise steadily in January 2008, the same year the financial crisis deepened around the globe. Hence, it is not surprising to see increasing volatility in exchange rate returns in the Post-period. This is in line with our results that the increased overall volatility comes from the new information.

Robustness Check

To control for the impact of the financial crisis between 2006 and 2009, we add an independent dummy variable named "financial crisis". To identify the financial crisis period, we use the spread between Libor and Overnight Indexed Swap (OIS) to proxy how severe the financial crisis was. Thus, we use a dummy variable with binary numbers 1 for the crisis period (September to December 2008) and 0 for the rest of the period

Table A1.10 GARCH (1,1) analysis for South Africa, impact of financial crisis
controlled

	Intercept (α_0)	ARCH (α_1)	GARCH (β_1)	$\alpha_1+\beta_1$	δ
Pre-Derivative	4.01e-06	0.0322642	0.9247918	0.957056	
P value	0.250	0.098	0.000	0.098	
Post-Derivative	0.000275	0.0720019	0.8662979	0.9382998	1.876881
P value	0.637	0.036	0.000	0.000	0.000

Table A1.11 GARCH (1,1) analysis for India, impact of financial crisis
controlled

	Intercept (α_0)	ARCH (α_1)	GARCH (β_1)	$\alpha_1+\beta_1$	δ
Pre-Derivative	–14.02913	0.1438344	0.8035084	0.9473428	2.168283
P value	0.000	0.000	0.000	0.000	0.000
Post-Derivative	3.08e-06	0.1259465	0.7386511	0.8645976	
P value	0.000	0.000	0.000	0.000	

between 2006 and 2009. Accordingly, the GARCH variance equation is
modified as follows.

$$\sigma_t^2 = \alpha_0 + \alpha_1\varepsilon_{t-1}^2 + \beta\sigma_{t-1}^2 + \delta DF \dots (4)$$

The empirical results after controlling for the crisis variable
are shown in Table A1.10. Compared with Table A1.9, the ARCH
coefficients and GARCH coefficients go in opposite directions:
The ARCH coefficients increase whereas the GARCH coefficients
decrease, suggesting that the volatility coming from the new information increases, while the volatility from the persistent old information decreases. Overall, the unconditional variance of the returns
decreases, which confirms our hypothesis that the increased overall
volatility was mainly caused by the global financial crisis. After controlling for this effect, the exchange futures market actually reduced
overall volatility, contrary to concerns that derivatives markets are
destabilizing.

For the robustness check, we also apply the financial crisis dummy for India, as the sample period ranging from January 2006 to December 2009 covers the financial crisis period. After introducing the financial crisis dummy in the variance equation for India, the results still hold for India (i.e., the introduction of the futures market reduced the overall volatility of the spot market). The results are shown in Table A1.11.

Appendix 2: An Overview of the International Foreign Exchange Futures Market

An overview of the FX derivatives markets in the US and Japan

The termination of the Bretton Woods system paved the way for the early development of the currency derivatives market in the US. Exchange rate volatility increased following the dissolution of the fixed exchange rate system, spurring demand for currency risk hedging. Early discussions about a currency futures market received mixed opinions, including many weighty objections. Milton Friedman offered his support in a short paper published at the end of 1971 that arguably established the intellectual foundation for a financial futures market. In his paper, Friedman summarizes the key rationales for developing a US-based currency futures market: promoting foreign trade and investment, strengthening the US financial services industry, reducing the volatility of cross-border capital flows, and facilitating the conduct of monetary policy.

Dollar-linked products dominate the global exchange-traded currency market. Trading in currency futures in the US remained relatively stable for most of the 1980s, followed by a contraction between 1999 and 2004 due to the introduction of the euro. Demand for currency futures regained momentum and experienced a period of explosive growth in the aftermath of the 2008 financial crisis due to heightened risk aversion and hedging needs. Overall, dollar-based currency futures account for the lion's share of the global exchange-traded currency futures (Figure A2.1).

Exchange-traded FX futures have always remained a small fraction of the wider over-the-counter (OTC) FX market in the US, but they have been critical in enhancing price discovery and providing market liquidity. Although exchange-traded futures boast many advantages over the OTC markets such as standardized products, high liquidity, long trading hours, transparency, and better regulation, they lack the

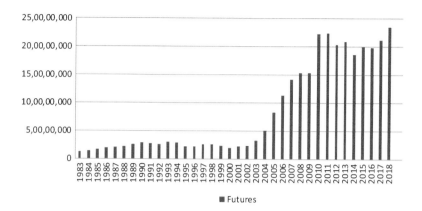

Figure A2.1 US: FX futures daily turnover (number of contracts).
Source: FOW.

flexibility needed to cater to the differentiated needs faced by the private sector. As such, the development of currency futures has always been accompanied by concurrent developments in OTC foreign exchange derivatives. As of 2016, the average daily turnover of the US OTC foreign exchange derivatives market stood at USD 1.27 trillion – a scale larger than the USD 117 billion daily turnover of exchange-traded US dollar futures.

Official currency futures trading in Japan did not take place until 1989, with the establishment of Tokyo Financial Exchange (TFX) under the Financial Futures Trading Law of Japan. However, trading in the JPY/ USD futures product was sluggish and volatile as a result of frequent changes to the terms of contracts and trading mechanisms, among other factors. Trading in currency futures products was terminated in 2005 and replaced by "click365", an electronic platform that supports margin trading[1] in exchange-listed daily foreign exchange products. The platform successfully attracted the interest of individual investors in Japan and has since witnessed rapid growth in foreign exchange margin trading volume.

OTC market dominates the Japanese FX market. The OTC FX derivatives market in Japan has grown more rapidly than the exchange-traded market over the last two decades. Average daily turnover has grown from USD 168 billion in 1995 to almost USD 400 billion in 2016. FX swaps and forwards are the major instruments in the OTC FX derivatives market (Figures A2.2 and A2.3).

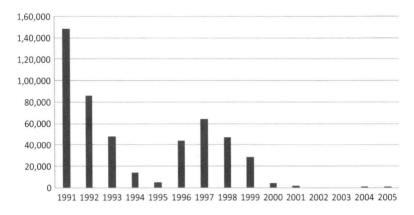

Figure A2.2 Japan: FX futures daily turnover (number of contracts).

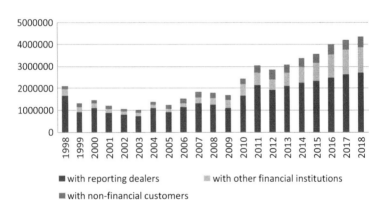

■ with reporting dealers   ■ with other financial institutions
■ with non-financial customers

Figure A2.3 Japan: Outstanding FX forwards and swaps by counterparty.
Sources: BIS, FOW and Bank of Japan.

Foreign Exchange Policies and the Foreign Exchange Futures Market in Brazil

Decelerating inflation and a stable exchange rate increased external borrowing and created demand for FX risk management. In 1994, Brazil introduced the Brazilian real as its new official currency as part of the Plano Real, which succeeded in bringing inflation down to the double-digit range. Yet despite active reform efforts, the monetary policy and exchange rate remained highly uncertain and volatile in Brazil prior to 1995. A surge in currency derivatives trading in 1994 and 1995 was, in part, driven by hedging needs as well as uncertainty over the newly adopted floating band. Starting in 1995, the floating band started to stabilize, and the exchange rate devalued steadily. The more stable exchange rate and high domestic real interest rate encouraged the private sector to shift toward low-cost foreign borrowing, resulting in the rapid buildup of external debt from 21.2% of GNI in 1995 to 43.1% of GNI[2] in 1999. The resulting exposure to external debt created incentives to use FX hedging instruments. The daily turnover of FX futures reached USD 2.3 billion in 1999 compared to USD 460 million in 1993.

The adoption of a free-floating exchange rate created long-term growth momentum for the FX derivatives market. Following the Russian debt moratorium in 1998, Brazil was seen as especially vulnerable given its arguably overvalued exchange rate, large current account deficit, and deteriorating fiscal position. In January 1999, the real was floated given continued pressure on the currency. Abandonment of the crawling peg led to a sustained growth momentum in FX futures trading, with trading volume growing tenfold between 1999 and 2008 and stabilizing at the same level thereafter.

Characteristics of the Brazilian FX derivatives market

The Brazilian FX futures market has four major characteristics. First, FX futures dominate Brazil's FX derivatives market. Unlike many countries such as the US where spot and OTC markets account for the lion's share of the FX market, Brazil boasts a well-developed futures market that takes a dominant position in the overall FX market. The dominance of the futures market stems partly from the tax and regulatory framework in Brazil that puts constraints on both the OTC and spot markets. The tax on revenues and cash flow, rather than income and value-added, creates a bias toward exchange-traded futures, where the purchases and sales of the same contract can be netted to reduce the amount of effective cash flow. Regulatory restrictions on the spot market also induce traders from the spot market to the futures market, where foreign exchange futures and options are non-deliverables and are settled in domestic currency. The main hedging instrument traded in the futures market is the DOL USD futures, with an average daily turnover of USD 16.3 billion in 2017 (Figure A2.4).

Second, the FX futures market plays a key role in price discovery. Given that the majority of foreign exchange transactions are conducted in the futures market, FX futures in Brazil serve a particularly important role in price discovery. According to Garcia, Medeiros, and Santos (2014),

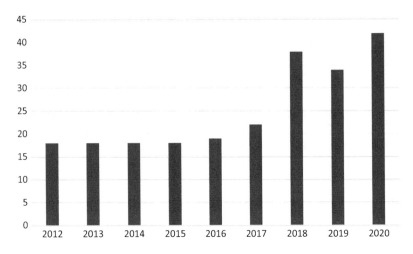

Figure A2.4 Trading volume of the Brazilian FX futures market.
Source: BIS.

the futures market in Brazil dominates price discovery as it responds to most of the fundamental price shocks and adjusts more quickly to the arrival of information. Price discovery transmits across the spot and futures markets via what is known as the *casado* transactions, which can serve to match positions across the two markets and eliminate arbitrage opportunities.

Third, most FX derivatives transactions are centrally cleared or reported. Central clearance and reporting requirements are well executed in the FX derivatives market. Exchange-traded futures contracts in Brazil are cleared via the BM&F central counterparty (CCP), while all OTC derivatives transactions are required to be reported to one of the two registration organizations – the BM&F and CETIP. The predominance of centrally cleared contracts and the reporting requirements reduce the buildup of counterparty risks while giving the authorities complete oversight of market activities, enhancing both transparency and systemic risk management.

Fourth, the Brazil Central Bank (BCB) has increased its presence in the derivatives market. Given its high liquidity and price discovery capacity, BCB's intervention in the FX market has increasingly shifted toward the derivatives market. Since the adoption of the floating exchange rate in 1999, BCB has frequently conducted auctions of domestic non-deliverable FX swaps to dealer banks in times of heightened exchange rate volatility. A domestic non-deliverable FX swap is essentially a USD forward contract that is settled in domestic currency. The instrument allows the central bank to take a short-dollar position in the market and provide FX hedging to the market. The settlement in domestic currency allows regulators to circumvent the need to tap foreign reserves directly, which serves to preserve foreign reserves in times of external turbulence. However, such an instrument carries the cost of rising public debt when positions taken by the central bank materialize into losses. From 2013 to 2015, the BCB carried out a major program of intervention in the derivatives market to stem volatility from the Federal Reserve's "taper tantrum", selling USD 115 billion worth of swaps to the market. At the peak of the program, the BCB accounted for almost half of the outstanding swaps and emerged as the major counterparty to the market.

Firms primarily use FX derivatives to hedge FX risks. The motives for firms to use FX derivatives vary. Using a sample of non-financial Brazilian firms, Junior (2007) found that firms' decision to use FX derivatives can be influenced by their FX exposure, the cost of hedging, exchange rate regime, and the probability of suffering financial distress. More specifically, firms with greater FX exposure in their cash flows and external debt make greater use of FX derivatives. Large companies are more inclined to use FX derivatives, suggesting that the cost of hedging matters. Exchange rate regime also plays a role, as evidenced in the upsurge of hedging activities after the adoption of the floating exchange rate in 1999. However, not all firms use FX derivatives for hedging purposes. Oliveira (2004) and Junior (2011) both confirmed the existence of a significant proportion of firms that speculate during times of heightened exchange rate volatility.

Management of FX risks has contributed to the mitigation of macro-financial risks, especially in times of economic stress. The well-developed and regulated FX derivatives market in Brazil has arguably played an important role in mitigating macro-financial stability risks during many episodes of economic turbulence, including the Asian financial crisis (1997), the Russian debt crisis (1998), the abandonment of the crawling peg (1999), the Enron bankruptcy and Argentine crisis (2002), the global financial crisis(2007), and the recent fiscal and political crisis (2015). The private sector was able to hedge its external liabilities and foreign cash flows by resorting to a wide range of hedging instruments. In times of extreme volatility, the authorities would step in as the hedger of last resort and provide market liquidity, essentially transferring foreign currency mismatch risks from the private sector to the public sector. Access to a variety of low-cost and liquid hedging vehicles has allowed the private sector to limit the impact of external volatility on their balance sheet and stay resilient against external shocks.

An Overview of India's FX Futures Market

The OTC FX market in India has expanded rapidly alongside financial liberalization. Trading in India's OTC FX market was negligible back in 1995 but has since grown to a daily turnover of USD 34 billion as of 2016.

The OTC market is dominated by FX forwards and swaps. FX forwards and swaps are the most actively traded derivatives instruments, accounting for more than half of the entire OTC FX market (Figure A2.5).

The very first rupee-dollar futures product was launched offshore on Dubai's Gold and Commodity Exchange (DGCX) in 2007. In the same year, the RBI convened a special research group to study international experiences in FX futures market development and to propose a suitable framework for the onshore FX futures market in India. In April 2008, the RBI joined with the Securities Exchange Board of India to grant permission for FX futures trading on the National Stock Exchange (NSE). The newly introduced FX futures had an impressive debut and have shown robust growth since their inception. As of 2018, the average daily turnover of rupee-based currency futures and options stood at around USD 1.2 billion, making the rupee one of the most liquid exchange-traded currencies globally. The most actively traded

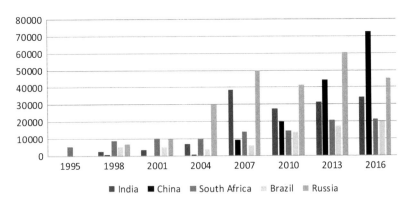

Figure A2.5 BRICS: OTC FX market daily turnover (millions of US dollars).
Source: BIS.

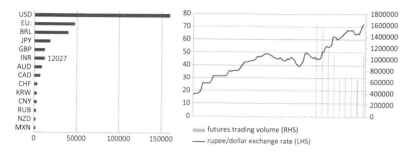

Figure A2.6 Trading volume of India's FX futures market: international comparison.
Sources: BIS, FOW.

products on the NSE are USDINR, GBPINR, and EURINR, with a concentration toward short maturities of one to two months or less (Figure A2.6).

Rupee-linked derivatives are traded both onshore and offshore via both exchanges and OTC. There are three onshore exchanges: the NSE, Bombay Stock Exchange (BSE), and Metropolitan Stock Exchange (MSE). Data on daily trading volume are publicly available on each exchange's website. Offshore exchanges that trade rupee-linked products include the CME, DCGX, and Singapore Exchange, with DCGX accounting for the largest share of trading activities (Figure A2.7).

Offshore trading accounts for a significant share of the rupee market. We estimate onshore and offshore trading volume in 2013 and 2016 by combining the BIS' database with statistics from the Indian exchanges.[3] The share of offshore exchange-traded derivatives expanded slightly, from about 40% in 2013 to about 43% in 2016. Meanwhile, the share of offshore OTC trading remained somewhat constant at around 41%. Although estimates of the share of offshore trading can vary depending on the sources of data and estimation methodology, the general observation is that offshore trading in rupee derivatives accounts for a significant share of the overall transaction of rupee derivatives.

The presence of a large offshore FX derivatives market can be of concern to policy makers for several reasons. First, a lack of transparency and regulatory oversight in the offshore OTC market may result in unchecked accumulation of financial risks that can spread to domestic markets. Second, a large and segmented offshore market may diminish the effectiveness of price discovery and, in the event of market stress, may be vulnerable to panic and liquidity constraints due to the absence

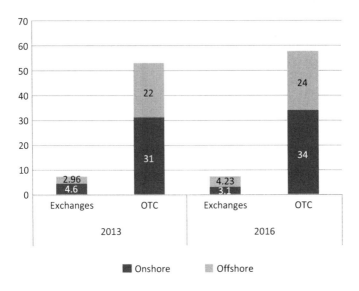

Figure A2.7 Onshore versus offshore rupee derivatives (average daily turnover, billions of US dollars).

Sources: BIS, NSE, MSE, and author's calculation.

of a central clearing platform. Last but not least, significant offshore trading increases the difficulty of capital flow management and FX intervention, especially for countries without a fully convertible capital account.

Capital restrictions, among other factors, have contributed to the large offshore market. A multitude of factors may have contributed to the presence of the large offshore rupee derivatives market. Restrictions on the capital account are an important factor, as both residents and non-residents with restricted access to the onshore derivatives market will resort to offshore instruments, such as NDFs, to manage FX risks. In the case of India, FIPs registered with SEBI have gained access to onshore currency derivatives since 2014, but are limited by their demonstrable positions in the equity and bond markets. Moreover, foreign investors in the onshore OTC market are restricted to a few selected custodian banks, imposing further limitations on their market options.

Competition from the offshore exchanges and dealers can also divert investors from onshore to the offshore market. The competitiveness of the offshore market can emerge in different forms, including higher position limits, faster registration with less onerous know-your-customer

(KYC) documentations, longer trading hours, and better legal and tax environment. The Indian authorities have taken steps to enhance the competitiveness of onshore markets, such as increasing position limits and proposing extended trading hours.

Finally, policy uncertainty can result in regulatory risks and fend off market participants with high risk aversion. In 2013, the RBI tightened capital control in response to the Federal Reserve's taper tantrum announcement and a depreciating rupee, including a ban on banks' proprietary trading in the currency futures exchange market.[4]

Russia: Committing to a Floating Exchange Rate Regime and Capital Account Convertibility Despite Adverse External Environment

The Russian economy experienced an abrupt downturn from 2014 to 2016, driven in part by falling oil prices, economic sanctions, tightening global liquidity, and lingering domestic structural issues. Real growth in Russia decelerated from more than 4% in 2010 to 0.7% in 2014, before turning negative in 2015 (-2.5%). The economic downturn was accompanied by a shrinkage in cross-border trade: import and export volume declined by 37% and 0.7% respectively from 2014 to 2016.

The sharp fall in oil prices in 2014 took its toll on the oil-dependent economy, especially on the export sector. Oil and mineral fuels export accounted for over 70% of Russia's exports prior to the crisis (2012 and 2013), contributing to a significant trade surplus in Russia. The sharp fall in oil prices from more than USD 100 per barrel to about USD 30 per barrel resulted in a significant decline in Russia's terms of trade. Many factors have contributed to the falling oil prices, including a slowdown in emerging market demand and an increase in oil production from the US and Canada.

Geopolitical tensions and economic sanctions exacerbated the recession. Following Russia's actions in Crimea, a number of countries imposed sanctions on Russian individuals and entities. The tensions heightened investment risks in Russia, which dramatically increased the external cost of borrowing for Russian banks and firms. The EU and the US sanctions in 2014 targeted large state-connected Russian banks and firms by limiting their access to international financial markets.

Despite an increase in domestic policy rate, capital outflows accelerated amid tightening global liquidity, a depreciating ruble, and high domestic inflation. The ruble came under severe pressure in 2014 due to balance of payment vulnerabilities. Domestic inflation soared due to the depreciating ruble and Russia's countersanctions that restricted imports.

The Central Bank of Russia (CBR) raised the policy rate from 5.5% to 17% in the second half of 2014 to stabilize devaluation and inflationary expectations, but was not effective in taming the surge in capital outflows. Net capital outflows reached a record high of USD 154 billion in 2014 (since its previous peak in 2008).

Russia maintained a managed floating FX regime from 1998 to 2005 while making significant progress on capital account liberalization. Russia adopted a managed floating FX regime following the government debt crisis in 1998. FX dynamics were largely market driven during this period, though the BoR intervened repeatedly in the FX market to limit excessive exchange rate movement that might threaten macroeconomic and financial stability. Although the exchange rate continued to be tightly managed through 2002–05, significant progress was made on capital account convertibility, with the last capital account restriction effectively removed in July 2006. In tandem with rising oil prices, the ruble experienced steady upward pressure. The BoR intervened frequently in the FX market to contain the ruble's appreciation.

Despite external economic turbulence, the BoR has stood firm on its move toward exchange rate flexibility. In 2005, the central bank of Russia introduced a dual-currency basket (USD and EUR) as the operational indicator for its FX market. Again, the aim was to smooth the volatility of the ruble exchange rate vis-à-vis other major currencies. Faced with large external shocks during the global financial crisis, the BoR fixed the width of the band for the dual-currency basket and set the rule for automatic shifts of the operational band based on the accumulated amount of the Bank of Russia's FX interventions. The fixed band was subsequently abandoned in 2010. The gradual move toward a more flexible exchange rate regime was intended to create favorable conditions for market participants to adjust to a fully floating exchange rate environment.

A free-floating FX regime was officially adopted in 2014. In November 2014, the Bank of Russia took another step toward a free-floating ruble by abolishing the dual currency soft peg, as well as automatic interventions. However, the BoR maintains the right to intervene in the FX market to mitigate financial stability risks.

The Russian economy rebounded quickly from the downturn, proving to be more resilient than expected to the oil price shock and economic sanctions. Growth rate was back in the positive region in 2017, while inflation was brought down to the single-digit range. The current account surplus subsided as the recovery eased import compression, while the financial account strengthened as investor confidence improved. The moderate impact of the dual shocks reflect a combination of effective policy responses, including the adoption of a free-floating exchange rate, inflation targeting, liquidity support and capital injection to the financial system, and limited fiscal stimulus.

The adoption of a free-floating exchange rate has played an important role in supporting the recovery, especially by contributing to the effectiveness of inflation targeting. A free-floating exchange rate has been found to be an important prerequisite for effective inflation targeting. The introduction of the free-floating FX regime in 2014 has allowed the BoR to strengthen its control over both interest rates and money supply by limiting its presence in the FX market. Effective control over monetary targets was critical in containing inflationary pressure. The BoR successfully brought inflation down from a high of 15% in 2015 to below 6% in 2016 and beyond. The success in taming inflation was quite remarkable considering the unfavorable external environment that the Russian economy faced: oil prices remained low at around USD 50 per barrel, while economic sanctions persisted throughout 2016.

Flexible exchange rate served as a shock absorber that stabilized the current account. REER depreciated by 16% in 2015 and 8.6% in the first half of 2016, which caused imports to decline but boosted export competitiveness. Imports fell by about 38% from 2014 to 2016, while exports remained relatively unchanged, contributing to a current account surplus during the crisis.

Limited scale of FXI prevented market panics stemming from the depletion of FX reserves. The adoption of a free-floating exchange rate reduced the central bank's presence in the FX market and ensured a comfortable level of Reserve Adequacy Ratio (RAR) in times of economic stress.

Notes

1 Margin trading refers to FX transactions in which a trader deposits a portion of margin deposit with a FX firm, and has the option to postpone settlement arbitrarily.
2 World Development Indicator.
3 Onshore exchange turnover is approximated by combining the average daily turnover of USDINR contract traded on the NSE, MSE, and BSE. Offshore exchange trading is estimated as the difference between BIS' turnover data on exchange-traded (rupee) products and onshore exchange trading turnover.
4 The ban was lifted on June 20, 2014.

Index

Printed in the United States
by Baker & Taylor Publisher Services